Dancing in the Clouds with the Rainbows

ISBN 978-1-63874-077-3 (paperback)
ISBN 978-1-63874-936-3 (hardcover)
ISBN 978-1-63874-078-0 (digital)

Christian Faith Publishing, Inc.
832 Park Avenue
Meadville, PA 16335
www.christianfaithpublishing.com

Printed in the United States of America

Dancing in the Clouds with the Rainbows

Janmarie Oakley

Dedication

To my husband, Jimmy, whose perseverance, character, encouragement, love and confidence in me; made this book possible. His life is an example of integrity and faith and I am truly blessed.

Above the Line

Set your mind on things that are above,
not on the things of this earth.

—Colossians 3:2

Living in today's world of technology and social media has made it more difficult to locate the lines in our lives. We have heard the statement, "This is where I draw the line," but oftentimes, we are unable to locate that line. Christ drew the line for us. Set your mind on things that are above, not on things that are below on earth. For most of us, we live below the line, focusing on the stuff of this world. Below the line are many things that hold our attention such as our careers, family, sports, social media, and yes, even our churches! We become consumed with activities, and our focus is on what we can do to be happy. Then we run into a roadblock—a financial crisis, broken relationships, critical illness or loss of a loved one—and we look below the line to find answers, and there are none. The answers in this life are only found above the line. Below the lines is greed, chaos, bitterness, anxiety, and hatred. Above the line is strength, joy, peace, and love.

Colossians 3:1 tells us we have been raised with Christ. Seek the things that are above. What would that be like? Instead of anger and conflict, peace. Instead of malice, good. Greed is replaced by contentment, and obscene language is replaced by edifying and praiseworthy language. Our human nature is to desire the things of this earth; however, to look above the line, we need to accept that this earth is not permanent. The psalmist in Psalm 103:15–16 writes:

> As for man his days are like grass; As a flower of the field, so he flourishes. For the wind passes over it and it is gone. And its place remembers it no more.

In 2 Corinthians 4:16, Paul writes to the church of Corinth, "So we do not lose heart, though our outward self is washing away, our inner self is being renewed day by day." We re new our inner selves by spending time with Our Lord, praising and praying. Choose to abide in Him and walk in the Holy Spirit. Living below the line is temporary and results in discontentment. Living above the line is permanent and results in true peace and eternal life.

> But seek first the kingdom of God and His righteousness. (Matthew 6:30)

The line is drawn. The choice is yours.

Cloud of Reflection

List things below the line that steal your attention.

Write a prayer asking the Lord to help you focus on the things above the line.

Antidote for Anxiety

Always be joyful. Never stop praying. Be
thankful in all circumstances for this is God's
will for you who belong to Christ Jesus.

—1 Thessalonians 5:16–18 (NLT)

The society we live in today is anxiety driven. Numerous factors in our daily lives cause us anxiety. Traffic, deadlines, financial challenges, health and family concerns are just a few. We are often thinking of what already happened or might happen. On days when I have a seminar presentation, I am always anxious. The inside of my stomach feels like butterflies fluttering from one anxious thought to another. What will I wear or what if the computer doesn't work right or maybe no one will attend are just a few of the thoughts racing through my mind. It is not always easy to wake up and say that I rejoice in this day that the Lord has made because we are focused on what happened yesterday or could happen today.

There are times in our life when we experience loneliness, failures, and disappointments. Habakkuk experienced experience this too and noted in Habakkuk 3:17–19:

> Even though the fig trees have no blossoms
> and there are not grapes on the vines, even though
> the olive crop fails and the fields be empty and
> barren; even though the flocks dies in the fields
> and the cattle barns are empty, yet I will rejoice
> in the Lord. I will be joyful in the God my salva-
> tion. The sovereign Lord is my strength.

Habakkuk knew the antidote to anxiety was His Lord.

Rejoice when our children take a road headed for destruction. Rejoice when our careers we have worked so hard at begin to crumble. Rejoice when death steals our child or spouse. Yes, rejoice, but let all who take refuge be thankful during the circumstance not for it and pray continuously. Trust God in difficult times and know that He will carry us through. One of Satan's most effective tools is to get us anxious and distraught so we are unable to focus on God's power and presence. The more we attempt to fix our circumstance, the more anxious we become. The psalmist declares in Psalm 5:11, "But let all who take refuge in you, rejoice: let them ever sing for joy."

Regardless of your circumstance, choose today not to worry. The most effective defense again anxiety and worry is continual communication with Our God. Anxiety will not change our circumstance, but God's presence and power can. When anxiety fills your soul like a poison, breathe in the antidote of joy.

Cloud of Reflection

List difficult circumstances in your life.

List your anxiety, then write a prayer thanking God for His power and grace.

Autumn Leaves

A time to keep, a time to cast away.

—Ecclesiastes 3:6

Fall—a time when the summer heat subsides, a time when our creation is alive with colors of orange, yellow, and reds on the trees, and a time of change, moving into the coolness of autumn. The leaves turn into vibrant colors before they fall to the ground.

A quote from Christian artist Toby Mac:

> The trees are about to show us just how beautiful it can be to let things go.

Most of us don't think letting go of things can be beautiful. We hold on tight as if to let go would be the end. We think if we hold on to that relationship or career, everything will eventually be okay, and we cannot imagine letting go. What if the trees refused to let go of their leaves of vibrant colors? If the tree didn't release the leaves, the tree would become unproductive, and in the spring would be bare of new growth.

What God has planned for us is never in the past. He has something better than that job or relationship, something greater than our fears and worries. The prophet Isaiah in Isaiah 43:18–19 (NLT) states, "But forget all that—it is nothing compared to what I am going to do. For I am about to do something new." Isaiah goes on to tell us that the Lord will make a path through the wilderness of your pain and failures. And where there is a drought, He will renew you with refreshing springs of life and new beginnings.

A quote from C. S. Lewis:

> Getting over a painful experience is like crossing monkey bars. You have to let go at some point to move on.

What are you holding on to today? Is it a broken relationship, a hurt, an unanswered prayer or a dream that is unattainable? Whatever it is, let it go. Cast it away. Paul wrote to the church in Philippi, "But one thing I do, forgetting what is behind and straining toward to what lies ahead" (Philippians 3:12–13). How different Paul's ministry would have been had he held on his past failures and hurts? Paul let it go and moved forward, sharing the mercy and love of our Lord Jesus Christ. His life is an example of letting go resulting in a beautiful life. Follow the example of the trees. Let it go and see the perfect and beautiful plan God has for you.

Cloud of Reflection

What are you holding on to today?

Write Philippians 3:12–13 on an index card and place in an area to remind yourself to move discard and move forward.

Be a Froot Loop in a Cheerio World

May the Lord direct your hearts to the love
of God and to the steadfastness of Christ.

—2 Thessalonians 3:5

In a society driven by instant gratification and competitive lifestyles, acts of kindness and grace are rare. We are commanded to love one another and to serve others. However, the society of today promotes the philosophy of "it's all about me." What if for one day every word you spoke and every action you performed was about someone besides you? Paul wrote to the Colossians in Colossians 4:6, "Let your speech always be gracious." When dealing with relationships that are difficult, it is easier to be unkind than gracious.

Social media promotes ungracious speech and unkind words. People think that it is okay to say whatever they think about a subject or person on Facebook, Instagram or Twitter without any regards to feelings or outcomes. We rationalize and say, "Well, that's the way things are done in the twenty-first century." No one escapes the wrath of others' opinions as evidenced by verbal attacks on our President of the United States, state governors, local authorities, athletes, movie actors or TV announcers to name a few. Think about how different our country would be if everyone seasoned their speech with grace and their actions with kindness. Instead of yelling or cutting off a driver who pulled in front of you, allow then to pull over with a smile.

The letter to the Philippians Paul wrote instructs Christians how we are to treat each other.

> Do nothing from selfish ambition or conceit, but in humility count others more significant than yourselves. Let each of you look not only to his own interests, but also to the interests of others. (Philippians 2:3–4)

Wow. Think of others more than myself? What a foreign concept in today's world! We live in a world full of Cheerios all seeking self-satisfaction and success without any regards to others. But what about the Froot Loops? They are bright and add character and smiles to life. It is easier in today's society to be a Cheerio than a Froot Loop; however, what a difference we can make in others' lives when we are the Froot Loops!

> Do not be conformed to this world, but be transformed by the renewing of your mind. (Romans 12:2)

My challenge for you today is to be a Froot Loop in a Cheerio world and be a light in someone's life!

Cloud of Reflection

Look for ways today to be a Froot Loop!

Being in the Now Moment

For all flesh is like grass and all its
glory like the flowers of the grass. The
grass withers and the flower falls.

—1 Peter 1:24

I absolutely love flowers! There's something special about a colorful bouquet, and regardless what kind of day I am having, they make me happy inside and smile. Pink daylilies, yellow roses, white gladiolus, and yellow daisies are just a few of my favorite combinations. While these colorful arrangements of blooms bring an uplift of the heart and mind. They don't last forever, that's why I place them in a vase where I can see them and enjoy all during the day. I call it "being in the NOW moment."

Our days are like grass of the field and wind passes over it and it is gone (Psalm 103:14). Hours, days, weeks, and months fly by. One day we are celebrating the new year, the next, school is out for the summer, and before we know it, we are Christmas shopping and decorating again. We plan parties, vacations, and family gatherings, focused on decorations, food, invitations, and making sure all the attendees are happy.

All that is good, except we oftentimes become so focus on the details that we miss the NOW moments. Luke recorded an example of missing this in the tenth chapter about Mary and Martha. Jesus comes to their house, bringing His disciples with Him. Martha was so distracted and focused on the details of serving everyone that she become frustrated with Mary who was sitting at the feet of Jesus, taking in every word He spoke. Mary was in the NOW moment. Martha asked Jesus to tell Mary to help, and His response was, "Martha,

Martha, you are worried and troubles about many things; But one thing is needed and Mary has chosen that good part, and it shall not be taken from her." (Luke 10:41–42)

Mary recognized the NOW moment and stopped and took advantage of it where Martha missed it because she was focused on details that in the end did not matter.

The same applies to us in our daily lives. How many NOW moments do we miss in a day or week because we are focused on details or moving on to something else? Now moments are everywhere if we stop to see them. A sunset, a child's laugh, a bouquet of flowers, and unexpected card in the mail, sitting on the beach watching the sand wash the shells in and out into the ocean are just a few. A call from an adult child just to say hi and not having a problem is a NOW moment.

God provides them all during our day, but the key is to stop and recognize them as Mary did. Celebrate today. Seize the NOW moments and bask in their joy.

> The heavens declare the glory of God and
> the firmament shows His handiwork.
>
> —Psalm 19:1

Cloud of Reflection

Look for the NOW moments this week and write them down and reflect on God's goodness.

Broken Crayons Still Color

The Lord is close to the broken hearted
and saves those who are close in spirit.

—Psalm 34:18

Who doesn't love a big box of new crayons all colorful, sharp, and ready to design whatever we want? I still love to color, especially with my granddaughter, and having a new box of crayons is a treat! However, as time progresses, the crayons become dull and broken. But just because the crayons are no longer bright, sharp, and new, it does not mean they will not color. In fact, they color just as well as before even if not as quickly. Does the picture look worse with broken crayons? No, of course not!

The same is true with our life. We start out our day fresh, bright and new, and ready to take on the world. But as the days go by, we can become broken and dull as a result of heartaches and disappointments. The loss of a loved one, a job promotion passed over, broken relationships, and health issues can break our spirit resulting in the inability to color our life as we want. When we are broken, our tendency is to quit and not complete the picture. What does the Bible say about being broken? In Zephaniah 3:17:

We are broken but God still takes great
delight in us. He rejoices over us with singing.

God loves us regardless of our failures and broken pieces in our lives. Paul tell us in the book of Romans that there is nothing we can do to separate us from the love of God.

When we are heart broken, it is essential to remember God's promises. God is near.

> The Lord is near to those who are discouraged; He save those who have lost all hope.
> (Psalm 34:18)

As children of the King, we have a high priest who understands our hurts, tears, and disappointments, and He is near. What a comfort to know that Our God does not leave us stranded in hopelessness and heartbreak! God is with us and will give us the strength we need.

> In the day when I cried out, You answered me, and made me bold with strength in my soul.
> (Psalm 138:3)

We are assured in Romans 8:18:

> For I consider that the sufferings of this present time are not worthy to be compared with the glory which shall be revealed to us.

As hard as our circumstances may be, they will not last forever. And one day in His kingdom, we will understand and see His glory in all that happened in our life.

Even when we are heart broken, we can still color, and God's everlasting presence is with us to guide and give us strength we need. We are all broken and live in a broken world, but just as broken crayons still color, so can we. We can color our life with God's fruits of the Spirit: love, joy, peace, longsuffering, kindness, goodness, faithfulness, gentleness, and self-control written in Galatians 5:22–23. So if your box of crayons today is broken, keep on coloring because Our Lord God is creating a master piece, and He will take your heartbreak and turn it into joy for His glory!

Through the Lord's mercies we are not
consumed, Because His compassions
fail not. There are new every morning;
Great is Your faithfulness.

—Lamentations 3:23

Cloud of
Reflection

Memorize Lamentations 3:23.

Bubbles

Let us hold fast the confession of
our hope without wavering; for
He who promised is faithful.

—Hebrews 10:23

"Bubbles, bubbles, and more bubbles." That is what my granddaughter would always say at bath time. She would cover herself with bubbles and wave them into the air, laughing continually. One of my favorite past time activities is dipping a wand into bubble solution, waving the bubbles into the air. Oftentimes, I sit at the pool or on the beach and watch them skip across the water. The bubbles reflect the sunlight and are light and airy as they float off into the sky without a care in the world. Life today in the hustle and bustle of the twenty-first century is a long ways from the carefree life of a bubble. How much easier life would be if we could dip a wand into a bottle of solution and wave our problems up into the air?

We have a tendency to think God is our bubble solution and Jesus is our wand to dip into when times are difficult. Our Lord Is not a genie; however, He provides us bubbles of His promises that do not float off into the sky. His promises are true and steadfast. When we face challenges and trials, we need to grab hold to His promises and apply them to our life.

In Deuteronomy 31:8, "It is the Lord who goes before you. He will be with you; he will not leave you or forsake you. Do not fear or be dismayed." Regardless of the circumstances in your life, God goes before you providing guidance through this situation. The psalmist writes, "Weeping may tarry in the night but joy comes in the morn-ing." (Psalm 30:5)

And another great promise is found in Lamentations 3:22–23:

> The steadfast love of the Lord never ceases,
> his mercies never come to an end; they are new
> every morning; great is Your faithfulness.

The only things steadfast in this world of today are chaos and change. What a comfort to know that our Lord God is steadfast regardless of our failures or the chaos that surrounds us. Our cir-cumstances may seem impossible, but His presence and power are steadfast. And in the impossible, Jesus tells us, "My grace is sufficient for you; for may power is made perfect in weakness." (2 Corinthian 12:9)

Life does not consist of bubbles floating off into the air; how-ever, as God's children, we have a hope and promise with Our Father in heaven that will not float off and leave us.

Cloud of Reflection

On an index card, write a promise for everyday and post where you can see it daily.

Bugs on My Windshield

This is the day the Lord has made,
we will rejoice and be glad in it.

—Psalm 118:24

The best part about a road trip is arriving to our destination without a disaster, safe and sound. However, regardless of the road we take, there will be bumps, unexpected curves, and yes, bugs on our windshield! In preparation for our road trip, we fill our gas tank and clean our windshield; however, regardless of how clean the windshield is before you reach the destination, it will be cluttered with bugs when you arrive. These bug splatters are not only annoying but makes it more difficult seeing the direction we need to go.

The same is true with this road trip we call life. We awake to a new day and prepare for it by getting showered and dressed. We start the day with a full tank and a clean windshield. Regardless as we travel through our day, our tanks become empty and our windshield splattered with bugs. So how do we respond when troubles splatter on our day, making it a challenge to travel the way we so carefully planned? Bugs of disappointments, illness, conflicts, and hurts splatter our day. Paul tells us in his letter to the Romans, "And I am convinced that nothing can ever separate us from God's love. Neither death, nor life, neither angels nor demons, neither our fears for today nor worries about tomorrow-not even the power of hell can separate us from God's love. No power in in the sky or the earth below, indeed, nothing in all creation will ever be able to separate us from the love of God that is revealed in Christ Jesus Our Lord" (Romans 8:38–39 NLT).

While the bugs are annoying and sometimes change our direction we are traveling, they cannot separate us from His power and love. The prophet Isaiah in Chapter 54, verse 10 said, "Though the mountains be shaken and the hills be removed, yet my unfailing love for you will not be shaken not my covenant of peace be removed; says the Lord who has compassion on you." So in spite of the bugs that splatter on your day, remember that God is faithful and He will not forsake us.

Jamie Grace's song entitled "Beautiful Day" reminds us that God has blessed us with a new day. "A day with sunshine on my face. And when troubles rain on my parade, let the rain wash the bugs from my windshield." A beautiful song about God's unfailing presence in our life even in the middle of bugs on our windshield! God's grace, His unfailing love, washes away the bugs maybe not as quick as we would like, but His love covers and conquers them all! So the next time your windshield becomes cluttered with bugs, and I am sure it will, remember that "This is the day the Lord has made and we will rejoice and be glad in it." Our Lord is able and will not allow the bugs to overcome us. He is the victory!

Cloud of Reflection

List some bugs on your windshield.

Write a verse praising God for His power.

Contagious

And may the Lord make your love for one
another and for all people grow and overflow,
just as our love for you over flows.

—1 Thessalonians 1:3

At the time of writing this, the word contagious is the most frequently used word in our society. The news is all about being contagious during this pandemic of COVID-19. Medical professionals and scientists all have a different opinion of when you are contagious with this virus. Contagious diseases such as flu, colds, and coronavirus spread from person to person and most frequently, in direct contact. Ways to prevent spreading germs and viruses are frequent and proper hand washing, staying home when sick, and wearing masks when you are in close contact with crowds of people.

The state of being contagious can be either good or bad. We think of being contagious with a disease is bad; however, what if we were contagious with good things? While the world is consumed with being contagious with COVID-19, we are, at the same time, being contagious with spreading fear and desperation. How much easier this journey would be if we became contagious with joy, love, and kindness?

As Christians, we are to be "contagious" for Christ and spread His love to others around us. The Apostle Paul wrote a letter to the congregation of a small church in the city of Thessalonica who was making a worldwide impact for Jesus Christ. Their love for Jesus was so contagious and infectious that they were known throughout the Roman Empire. Paul wrote in verse three, "We recall, in the presence of our God and Father; your work produced by faith, your labor motivated by love and your endurance inspired by hope in our Lord Jesus Christ." Paul stated that because the congregation became imitators of Christ, God's word spread throughout the city. Wow! That's the kind of contagious we need to be, especially during this time when illness, fear, and chaos are being spread more than love, peace, and kindness. We need to produce and spread the fruits of the spirit, which are written by Paul in Galatians 5: 22–23:

> But the fruit of the Spirit is love, joy, peace, patience, kindness, goodness, faithfulness, gentleness and self-control.

The fruit of the Spirit refers to behavior produced by the Spirit of God and evidence that we belong to Christ. Spending time in His presence, reading His Word, and praying enable us to become imitators of Christ and produce qualities that reflect Him.

I challenge you to become contagious for Christ and spread His love to others around you. Who can refuse to smile back at a person who smiles at you? It hardly ever happens. You just can't help but smile back. In the same way, when we spread kindness, patience, love, and joy, it is difficult for others to refuse. Today, in this contagious world of viruses, chaos, hate, and fear, be the one who spreads hope, joy, and love.

Cloud of Reflection

Write down three things you can be contagious for and practice them daily.

Count Your Rainbows, Not Your Thunderstorms

The Lord is good to all and His
mercy is over all He has made.

—Psalm 145:9

Rainbows or thunderstorms? Pretty easy choice. Most of us would want the rainbows. The bright happy colors of the rainbow is a far better choice than the dark heavy clouds. However, life does not give us a choice. There are days that are bright and happy, and others, we struggle to stay afloat the rough waves and dark clouds. God's word in 1 Thessalonians 5:18:

In everything give thanks, for this is the will
of God in Christ for you.

Really? Give thanks for the critical health issue or the broken relationship? Yes, in everything, give thanks—rainbows and thunderstorms. When we have days of rainbows, it is easy to take for granted what we have. The society we live in is focused on what we can obtain next—a better job, new car, new house or a luxury vacation. On days when we have the thunderstorms and the thunder is so loud, we cannot think or hear. We tend to focus only on the storm and forget about all the blessings we have. God wants our praise during the storm.

One of my favorite songs by Casting Crowns is "Praise Him During the Storm." The words of chorus are, "And I will praise You

26

in this storm. For You are who you say You are." He is Lord God, creator of the earth.

> He covers the heavens with clouds. He prepares rain for the earth. He makes the grass to grow on the hills. (Psalm 147:8)

His love is steadfast, reaching to the heavens and His faithfulness to the clouds.

In the storm, we need to remember our rainbows, our blessings. Psalms 103:2, "Bless the Lord, O my soul. And forget not His benefits." What are His benefits? Forgiveness of our sins, healing from our illnesses, saving us from the pit, providing us with His steadfast love and mercy, and renewal daily with good things. What an awesome God we serve. And regardless of the thunderstorms, we have His protections and faithfulness. Only our God can make new beginnings from unhappy endings. It is much easier to ride out the storm with our focus on the rainbows instead of the thunder. Maybe today you are in a thunderstorm, and if you are not, get ready because one is on the radar. Praise Him. Count your rainbows. It is good to give thanks to the Lord for all He has provided us.

Cloud of Reflection

List your rainbows.

Dancing in the Shadow

He who dwells in the shelter of the Most High
will abide in the shadow of the Almighty.

—Psalm 91:1

Do you remember as a child chasing your shadow as dusk drew near? I remember playing on our front yard with my sisters making dramatic movements with our arms and legs and watching as our shadow danced. We were not afraid of our shadows. We knew they were safe.

As children of God, we are protected by His almighty shadow. Our key verses tell us in order to have protection, we must dwell in the presence of our Lord God. David cried out to the Lord in Psalm 57:1:

> Be merciful to me, O God, be merciful to me! For my soul trusts in You; And in the shadow of Your wings I will make my refuge, Until these calamities have passed by.

And in the familiar passage of Psalm 23:4:

> Yea though I walk in the shadow of death, I will fear no evil for you are with me and your rod and staff will comfort me.

Our shadows have no real purpose for us; however, the shadow of our Lord provides shelter from the rain and fear. He is our refuge in the present help of trouble. During difficult times, our hope is in the shadow of the Almighty. Even in trials of darkness, despair, and fear, we can sing His praises in His shadow. I love this verse, "Because You have been my help, Therefore in the shadow of Your wings I will rejoice." (Psalm 63:7)

We have a choice to take refuge either in the solutions of the world or to trust the One who is able to do the impossible.

> Now to Him who is able to do exceedingly abundantly above all that we ask or think according to the power who works in us. (Ephesians 3:20)

When the trials arrive and fear hovers over us and the pain is so intense we cannot breathe, go to Our Heavenly Father and rest in His shadow and dance in His presence. Take refuge in His power, joy and peace.

Isaiah 51:15–16:

> I am the Lord Your God. And I have put my words in your mouth; I have covered you with the shadow of My hand.

Cloud of Reflection

Journal a time when you rested in the shadow of God.

Delightful Living

Take delight in the Lord and He will
give you the desires of your heart.

—Psalm 37:4

Webster defines "delight" as to experience pleasure and gratification. The Hebrew term for delight is "hepes," meaning to be inclined to and "rasa," which is to delight and take pleasure in. To delight in something is to savor in it. Our hearts are a marketplace for all kinds of desires. We desire wealth, happy homes, successful careers, luxury vacations, and healthy life. We desire a problem-free life that provides us with pleasure and gratification, which oftentimes controls our thoughts and choices.

Our key verse tells us that we are to delight in the Lord, and He will give us the desires of our heart. That does not mean that the Lord is our genie in a lamp or Santa Claus. We don't just put in our desires like we insert coins in a vending machine.

A sunset is one of God's awesome creations. As we observe the sky explode with colors of orange, red, yellow, blue, and gray, as the sun slips into the horizon, we desire to stay in that moment, enjoying every part of the sunset. The same should be true when we are in the presence of Our Heavenly Father. We want to continue in His presence, soaking in His mercy, joy, and peace. The psalmist says, "So I have looked for You in the sanctuary. To see Your power and Your glory." (Psalm 63:2) Searching for the Lord, savoring His power and glory is to delight in Him.

In this broken world we live in, it is easier to delight or focus on our heartbreak and to wrongs that happen to us, sometimes by our own doing and often times by others. This kind of delighting destroys our soul and heart. There is no power when we delight in hurts and evil. However, delighting in the Lord regardless of our situation changes our perspective. Spending time in His sanctuary allows Him to guide us. In His sanctuary is grace, joy, and strength. The first chapter of Psalms verses one to three tells us that the one who is happy and does not walk in advice with the wicked but instead delights in the Lord's instruction and meditates on it day and night. And the result? He is like a tree—strong and firmly rooted and bears fruit and prospers. We may not delight in the circumstance, but we can delight in what the Lord will do. Delight produces trust.

What are you delighting in today? Is it a past hurt or disaster or is it the Lord God Almighty? In Him is grace, mercy, joy, and peace. And when we delight in Him, He will give us the desires that are everlasting and glorifying to Him.

Cloud of Reflection

What desires do you delight in?

Write a prayer asking the Lord to help you delight in Him.

Even If... When the What If's Happen

Then you will call upon Me and go and
pray to me and I will listen to you.

—Jeremiah 29:12

Thinking and worrying about the what-if's in life is similar to a STOP sign in which they bring us to a complete halt. Our focus on the what-if's rob us of the peace and joy of the present. What if the stock market crashes, what if we have a world war or what if a natural disaster destroys our home are just a few examples. When my husband and I retired and moved to a new location in a new house, my mind was constantly thinking about the what-if's. What if the new house isn't finished on time or what if we don't like our new location or what if one of us becomes terminally ill? All of these and many more spent a lot of time inside my head. Fear of the future, the what if's, can immobilize our spiritual growth.

Second Timothy 1:7:

For God has not given us a spirit of fear but
of power and of love and of sound mind.

However, there are times in our life that the what-if's occur, and our fears become our reality. It could be a diagnosis of cancer or broken relationships or financial crisis. In the gospel of John 11:1–27 is a story about when the what if's happen. It is the story of Lazarus, brother

32

of Mary and Martha. Lazarus was extremely ill, and his sisters sent a message to Jesus to come because their brother was sick. When Jesus arrived in Bethany, Lazarus was already dead. Martha went to Jesus and said, "Lord, if you had been here, my brother would not have died."

Martha's fear of what if Lazarus would die happened, and yet she said to Jesus in verse twenty-two, "But even I know that whatever you ask of God, God will give you." In the middle of the storm, Martha knew Jesus had the power to save Lazarus. Martha had faith that God was able and powerful in spite of the circumstance. How do you respond when your what if's become a reality? Do you have a faith like Martha and know that God is all powerful and in control and whatever His will is what will happen?

One of the most powerful Christian songs sung by Mercy Me is "Even If." The song talks about how easy it is to have faith when life is good; however, when difficulties come, it is harder to have faith and say it is okay. The chorus says, "I know You are able and I know You can, Save through the fire with Your mighty hand. But even if You don't, my hope is in You. But God when You choose to leave the mountains unmovable. O give me the strength to sing. It is well with my soul."

Whatever storm you are facing today, release to the One who is able. Have a Martha-like faith that regardless of the circumstance, you know that God is in control. Even if the what-if's happen, turn to the One who is all powerful and always faithful. And in the middle of the storm, you will experience peace.

You will keep the mind that is
stayed on You in perfect peace.

—Isaiah 26:3

Cloud of
Reflection

Do you have a what-if in your life today? Write a prayer asking the Lord to help you say, "Even if…it is well with my soul."

Everlasting Love

I have loved you with an everlasting
love, therefore I have continued to
extend faithful love to you.

—Jeremiah 31:3

The most accurate statement about our world today is that it is constantly changing. We are obsessed with technology and gadgets. We finally get the newest iPhone, and within months, a more efficient version is released. Our environment is in continual change as evidenced by erratic and unpredictable weather patterns. Extreme patterns such as blizzards, floods, wild fires, and drought occur often all over our world. One day, it is 90 degrees and sunny, and the next, it is 50 degrees and cloudy.

We experience constant motion in our daily lives—job changes, health issues, broken relationships for just a few. Life-changing events often produce doubt, fear, and uncertainty. We usually never see these trials coming, and we are knocked down and unsure what to do next.

Nothing is everlasting in our lives. The psalmist in Psalm 103:16–17 wrote:

> As for man his days are as grass, he flourishes like a flower of the field, for the wind passes over it and it is gone and its place knows it no more. But the steadfast love of the Lord is from everlasting to everlasting on those who fear Him.

I worked for thirty-three years in a long-term care facility and have witnessed a variety examples of everlasting love. One of my favorites is about a sweet man known as Dr. B. He came every day to the facility to see his lovely bride. She was confined to a wheelchair and unable to move without assistance. Mrs. B seldom participated in activities or socialized with other residents but, the minute her husband walked in, her entire face lit up in a beautiful smile. She would start talking the best she could within the limitations of dementia. The staff would transfer her to the sofa in her room, and the couple would sit together watching Fox News.

Mrs. B would put her head on his shoulder and oftentimes fall asleep. This was a daily occurrence regardless of the weather or his health issues. One day, I commented on how faithful he was, and I'll never forget his response to me. "I told her I would love her forever, and nothing has changed that!" Everlasting love. And Our Heavenly Father has told us that He will always love us, and nothing we can do can change that. In spite of our failures and weaknesses, He continues to be faithful.

Isaiah 54:8:

> But I will have compassion on you with an
> everlasting love.

What an assurance to know that in a world in constant change, Our God never changes. He is always faithful, and His love is everlasting. Maybe your life today is calm or maybe you are facing a storm. No matter the circumstances, think on His faithfulness and everlasting love.

> Give thanks to the God of gods, for
> His steadfast love endures forever.
>
> —Psalm 136:2

Cloud of
Reflection

Write down example of God's everlasting love that he has shown you.

Reflect on His faithfulness.

Faith with Muscle

Faith means being sure of the things we
hope for and faith means knowing that
something is real even when we do not see it.

—Hebrews 11:1

Across the United States, millennials are exercising more than ever. In 2017, statistics showed that sixty-four million Americans belong to a fitness center. The yellow pages as of January 1, 2017, listed 36,180 centers. Regardless of the age or social status, Americans are exercising and building their strength.

One summer, we visited Muscle Beach in Santa Monica, California. The outdoor gym was out in the middle of the boardwalk of Venice Beach. Men and women performed their workout for all to observe. It was quite impressive watching them with their muscular lean bodies lift heavy weights high above their heads and grab a bar and flip into the air. However, to have achieved this high-performance level and muscular body, it did not occur overnight. This took months and probably years of physical training. The training also included the proper nutrients to fuel the muscles, and my friends, that is not hamburgers, fries, and shakes. The majority of people who work out today are not trying to achieve this high level of workout but just trying to build strength and endurance for a healthy lifestyle. The results of regular exercise is a healthier body and a stronger heart.

Living today in our world requires a faith with muscle, which is only possible with a strong spiritual heart. A spiritual heart becomes strong by spending time in God's Word and prayer. Coping in a world of continual change requires a strong faith. We live life like we are in control of it and the people we hold dear. We plan our children's future and think we can protect them from evil and tragedies.

Americans spend hours planning our careers, vacations, and retirements. When the unexpected happen such as a job loss, terminal illness or a natural disaster, we are out of control and overwhelmed. The unexpected leaves us unsure of what direction to pursue. Our Lord is never surprised at the unexpected and always in control. During these times of difficulties, we need to have faith in the One who is all powerful. To live out life in fear produces chaos and turmoil; however, to live by faith produces peace. Instead of manipulating and attempting to change the outcome, we need to release them to Our Heavenly Father.

It is interesting how easily we trust the everyday things in our lives. For example, when you turn on the light switch, are you unsure that the lights won't come on? We never think about what if the lights do not come on. We enter a code into our security system and feel completely safe. I think we agree that our God is more powerful than man-made technology.

A muscular faith requires reading God's Word, praising Him, and praying. Spending time in the presence of our Lord builds a strong heart muscle. All things are possible with God.

> And without faith it is impossible to please Him. Anyone who wants to come to Him must believe that God exists and that He rewards those who sincerely seek Him. (Hebrews 11:6 NLT)

> For God has not given us a spirit of fear but of power and might. (2 Timothy 1:7)

Thomas Manot stated:

> What an excellent ground of hope and confidence we have when we reflect upon these three things in prayer: the Father's love, the Son's merit and the Spirit's power.

Start flexing your faith muscle. Start your faith workout today!

Record a verse that related to faith and journal what it says to you.

Fill Up Your Tank

And take the helmet of salvation and sword
of the spirit which is the word of God.

—Ephesians 6:17

The expression to 'fill up your tank' was used many years ago on a commercial advertising breakfast cereal. Tony the Tiger for Kellogg's Frosted Flakes would say, "Put a tiger in your tank," to start and have a great day! Breakfast has been documented as being the most important meal of the day and the key to you being mentally sharp and focused. While it may be true in relation to physical well-being that breakfast is the most important meal of the day, for our spiritual well-being, the most important thing to start our day is to spend time with our Lord, to fill our tank with His Word and presence. In the gospel of John chapter 21, we read about Jesus appearing to the disciples after being resurrected. In verse 12, Jesus said to them, "Come have breakfast." The disciples had been fishing all night, and Jesus met them on the shore and took bread and the fish and said it's time to have breakfast.

So what exactly does it mean to fill our tank with Jesus? In the book of Ephesians chapter 6, Paul gives instructions to the Ephesians on how to fill their tanks spiritually. Verses 10 and 11 tell us to "be strong in the Lord and to put on the whole armor of God." So what does the armor of God consists of?

The first thing we put on is the belt of truth. In the world we live today, truth is not popular. We see examples in our sports, politics, and careers daily how the truth is not told. Some days it is hard to know which is a lie or a truth. We as nation have deceived ourselves in thinking the truth is to take prayer out of school or to remove "In God we trust" off our money. Satan is the father of lies and deceit.

The second is to put on the breastplate of righteousness. While we are sinners, through salvation and belief in Jesus Christ, we are righteous in God's eyes. Applying the breastplate of righteousness is to strive to live a holy life, one that is pleasing to God. The third item is to put on your feet the Gospel of peace and to be grounded in the foundation of God's peace. We are to put on the shield of faith to fight against the evil one. And our key verse today says to put on the helmet of salvation, which is the Word of God. When we start our day with God's word, His truth, and apply it to our daily lives so we can be more righteous, then our tank is filled correctly. We are able to fight off the evil in this world and the unexpected turns that are often destructive.

I challenge you to "come have breakfast" with the Lord first in the morning and not check your phone for the latest social media happenings or news breaks. In order to be ready for whatever is in front of you, we must be spiritually ready and alert.

> Rejoice always, pray without ceasing, give
> thanks in all circumstances, for this is the
> will of God in Christ Jesus for you.

> —1 Thessalonians 5: 16–18

Cloud of Reflection

Start each morning with at least one verse or devotional.

Five Star Living

I have come that they may have life, and
that they may have it more abundantly.

—John 10:10

Five star living. Oh yes, that gets our attention. Hotels have a rating system using stars to indicate the level of service ranging from one to five. One star is budget basic needs; two is basic needs; three is a higher level of service and a few amenities; four star is superior property and guest services; and five is luxury services with a large variety of amenities. My husband says that I count the number of stars before I book a hotel. The way I see it, the more stars, the better. When we retired, we relocated to an area at Lake Lewisville. The advertising slogan says, "Are you ready to live resort-style?" Well, of course. Aren't we all?

Not everyone is able to choose five-star hotels and live resort-style; however, as children of the King, we are able to live resort-style and five-star living. I composed a list of just as few examples of five-star living as God's children.

Hope in a hopeless world. We have a hope that will never fail us.

Now hope does not disappoint, because the
love of God has been poured out in our hearts by
the Holy Spirit who as given to us. (Romans 5:5)

May the God of hope fill you with all joy and peace in believing,
so that by the power of the Holy Spirit you may abound in hope."

Love is an everlasting faithful unconditional love from Our Heavenly Father.

> This is real love, not that we loved God, but
> that He loved us and sent His son as a sacrifice to
> take away our sin. (1 John 4:10 NLT)

Another example of five star-living is joy. We often mistake joy and happiness for the same thing. True joy from the Lord is an everlasting joy that is not based on our circumstances.

Psalm 16:11:

> "You make known to me the path of life, in
> Your presence there is fullness of joy."

And in Nehemiah 8:10b:

> The joy of the Lord is my strength.

Regardless of the circumstance you are in, when you abide in Jesus, we have the joy to sustain us and carry us through.

Righteousness is being made right thru the power of Jesus Christ.

> For our sake he made him to be sin who
> knew no sin, so that in him we might become the
> righteousness of God. (2 Corinthians 5:21)

We are justified so we can become heirs of the King. To consider myself as righteous is quite difficult for me because Satan wants us to continually remember all of our past failures. But if we believe that God's word is true, then you must accept that we are made righteous when we have accepted Him as our Lord and Savior. Not only our sins forgiven but forgotten as far as the east is from the west.

The last star on my list is peace. Oh, how we all long and search for peace in our lives. The days on this earth are filled with chaos, heartbreak, and conflicts. The psalmist in Psalm 29:11b writes, "The Lord will bless His people with peace."

And in Isaiah chapter 26:3:

> You will keep him in perfect peace whose
> mind is stayed on you, because he trusts in you.

There are many stars in resort-living with the King. Other religions cannot offer five star living. The only true five star living is to have Jesus Christ as Lord and Savior. Today choose to live resort-style with the Lord.

Cloud of Reflection

Make your own list of five-star living and write an explanation of what each one means to you

Follow the Instructions

Those who listen to instruction will prosper,
those who trust the Lord will be joyful.

—Proverbs 16:20 (NLT)

Venice Beach Boardwalk in California is one of the most entertaining places I have visited. We found a skateboard park and observed an instructor teach a class of young boys the technique of skateboarding. The instructor called out instructions, "Turn your shoulders to the right. Move your feet clockwise or keep your head up." The boys would twist and turn as they went up and over the concrete hills. When they skated into the valleys of concrete, the instructor would call out for them to tuck their arms close to their body to build up speed to climb the hills. It was intriguing to watch the boys go up and down the hills and twist and fly into the air as the instructor coached them. One thing I noticed that as long as the students acknowledged the instructor and followed his instructions, they completed the circuit successfully. However, when they began to go their own directions, they quickly crashed to the concrete.

Our daily lives are similar to the skateboarders. We face hills, sharp turns, and valleys. There are unexpected events: loss of a job or a natural disaster. One minute we are twisting and flying in the air without any difficulty until suddenly, there is a sharp turn such as a terminal health diagnosis, financial crisis or loss of a loved one, and we crash to the bottom. These significant life events always hit us without warning. However, in this crisis, we have an instructor who knows which way we should go. Stop and listen for His instruction.

> I will instruct you and teach you in the way
> you should go. I will guide you with my eye.
> (Psalm 32:8)

Tuning in to our instructor is the key. He has the answers and knows the best way for us. Our God is with us just as he was with the children of Israel.

> The Lord went ahead of them. He guided
> them during the day with a pillar of cloud,
> and provided light at night with a pillar of fire.
> (Exodus 13:21)

We do not have a pillar of cloud or fire, but we have His Word. The skateboarders wore helmets and pads to protect their bodies. We, too, must put on the helmet of faith and the pad of God's Word to guide and protect us.

> I have set the Lord always before me because
> He is my right hand, I shall not be shaken. (Psalm
> 16:8)

Spending time in God's Word will provide us direction and wisdom.

> All scripture is inspired by God and is useful
> to teach us whet is true and to make us realize
> what is wrong and teach us to do what is right. (2
> Timothy 3:16 NLT)

When you are faced with the sudden sharp turns and hills on this life's journey, lift your head and tune in to the greatest instructor of all.

Cloud of
Reflection

Reflect on an area in your life you need God's instruction. Journal a prayer asking for guidance.

From Bulbs to Blooms

The Lord is good to those who wait for
Him; to the soul who seeks Him. It is good
that one should hope and wait quietly.

—Lamentations 3:25–26

One of my favorite things to do in the spring is plant flowers. Our lake house sidewalk is lined with marigolds and planters of zinnias. But my favorite of all are the caladiums. The back of our log cabin and the walkway to the water is lined with an array of pinks, reds, and white leafs. Several years ago, I found a place called Happiness Farm in Florida, which is one of the largest caladium farms in the US. I prefer to order a variety bag of pinks, reds, and whites, and Happiness Farms delivers the bulbs at the appropriate time to plant in your specific region.

The caladiums are carefully packed in crates of sawdust. After preparation of the soil, I arrange the bulbs in an orderly fashion on top of the soil and then push each bulb two to three inches into the soil. The hardest part of this process is waiting for the bulbs to sprout and burst into a colorful bloom. No shortcut is available, and nothing I can do can speed up the process. In approximately three weeks, the bulbs will push through the soil in a beautiful bloom in their own timing, regardless that they were all planted at the same time.

We all have bulbs in our life that we are waiting to burst into blooms. Perhaps it is a broken relationship, career challenges, health issues, and financial concerns. Our human nature is for these areas to be resolved quickly into blooms—right now, not tomorrow or next week or next year. As our impatience mounts, we search for shortcuts. We seek out counselors and self-help books to fix our relationships. We look to financial advisors to resolve our financial challenges. Medical technology today is remarkable, and we expect it to heal our health issues.

Isaiah 55:8:

> "For my thoughts are not your thoughts,
> neither are your ways my ways," declare the Lord.

The Lord declares it, but we have a difficult time accepting it. We cannot accept that our way could be wrong. Our Father in heaven knows the best way and is always working.

> It is God who works in you both to will and
> do His good pleasure. (Philippians 2:13)

God knows and understands our difficult situations, and He is able to take it and bring it to full bloom in His perfect way and time.

> As for God, His way is perfect and the word
> of the Lord is proven. (1 Samuel 22:31)

There is no bulb of difficulty that God cannot bring to a full bloom.

> Our God is able to do exceedingly abundantly above all that we ask or think according
> to the power who works in us. (Ephesians 3:20)

Cloud of Reflection

Write down an area in your life that is a bulb.

Write a prayer releasing them to God.

God Confidence

For He who promised is faithful.

—Hebrews 10:23b

We trust a variety of sources and people in our lives. Some are faithful, and some are not. Some people make promises and keep them, while others fall short. However, our Heavenly Father is always faithful to His promises. He promises to guide, protect, and love us unconditionally. Others may promise us security, stability, and love, but the human nature is oftentimes unable to fulfill those promises. We see examples of unfulfilled promises in this world of ours such as politicians make promises for lower taxes and a better country they are unable to fulfill and the weatherman promises a day of sunshine, and a storm pop ups. Our children promise to have a good day in school as they leave, and a few hours later, the teacher calls. And there is the spouse who promised to love for better or worse and decides to leave.

Our world is a world of broken promises. The first broken promise recorded is found in the book of Genesis chapter 3 when Eve eats the forbidden fruit, and Adam follows. We live in a world of broken promises; however, we have hope because the creator of this world is faithful and keeps His promises. God promised Noah never again to destroy the earth with a flood. And the ultimate promise is that whoever believes in Jesus Christ will not perish but have everlasting life. Regardless of our broken promises to Him, He is faithful and steadfast.

During times in in our life when we are disappointed and heart-broken, we have the promises of God to sustain and anchor us.

> The Lord will fight for you. You need only
> to be still. (Exodus 14:14)

And prophet Isaiah wrote in chapter 40, verse 31:

> But those who wait on the Lord shall renew
> their strength.

And Isaiah 41:10:

> Fear not for I am with you; Be not dis-
> mayed; for I am with you. I will strengthen you;
> Yes I will help you; I will uphold you with My
> righteous right hand.

When we focus on His promises, we receive His peace. Remember the One who never fails or breaks a promise during the days your dreams and promises are broken. Our God has a plan, and His plan is not our plan.

> For my thoughts are not your thoughts; not
> my ways your ways. For my ways are higher than
> your ways. (Isaiah 55:8–9)

Fix your eyes on Jesus and dwell in His promises. Have God confidence, not worldly confidence. God confidence is success, not failure.

> The steadfast love of the Lord never ceases,
> His mercies never come to an end.
>
> —Lamentations 3:22

*Cloud of
Reflection*

List seven promises from God on an index card, one for each day of
the week.

Place where you can read them daily.

God's Watercolor Palette

I will meditate on the glorious splendor of
Your majesty, And on Your wondrous works.

—Psalm 145:5

Lord God, creator of this universe daily, creates masterpieces of art for our pleasure. I continue to be amazed at the beauty of the sunrise and sunset. God takes His palette of colors and spreads them across the night sky in an array of oranges, yellows, and reds. The earth is still slumbering, and Our Creator sends a wake-up call of color from His palette, inviting us to start a new day. The sunrise is a grand entrance into a new beginning. Oftentimes we are so involved in getting up and ready for the day, we give little attention to God's masterpiece. The sunrise with all the bright colors spread across the sky reminds us that God is in control and will not forsake us.

Then at the end of the day, as the sun sinks into the earth, God provides us another masterpiece of His artwork. As the sun begins to go down, the bright colors of red and yellow fill the dusk sky. Regardless of the kind of day we have experienced, the Lord God reminds us with His palette of colors that He is still with us. This day is done, and He is still in control and sovereign. At the end of the day, you may be too weary to enjoy the gift of the sunset. Stop and enjoy God's beauty. What a refreshing gift after a long day. Since retirement, I have made it a priority to watch more sunrises and sunsets. When I gaze upon the sky filled with vivid colors, I praise Him for his creation, His holiness, and faithfulness.

God's watercolors of the sunrise remind me of a new start, bright and promising, regardless of the day before. And His sunset of colors reinforce that He is still with me—a beautiful ending regardless of the circumstances in my life.

> O Lord, our Lord, how majestic is
> your name in all the earth. You have
> set your glory above the heavens.
>
> —Psalm 8:1–2

*Reflection
Cloud*

Watch a sunrise or sunset and journal what God is saying to you.

GPS: Recalculating

In all your ways acknowledge Him and
He will make your paths straight.

—Proverbs 3:6

GPS is the abbreviation for Global Positioning System. GPS units receive signals for US satellites to determine location. GPS are versatile and found in almost every industry. They are used to map forests and oceans and navigate airplanes on the ground or in the air and provide directions to a specific location. GPS is available to anyone and is free of charge. One of the apps I use the most is the Navionics boat app to assist us on the lake and provides information regarding depth and location. We recently relocated to the Dallas-Fort Worth area, and my GPS has been working overtime. I just plug in the address and proceed; however, if I miss a turn, the voice on the GPS states, "Recalculating and gives a new set of directions."

Christians have a navigational system: The Bible, God's Word. His Word provides us with directions to eternal life and peace.

I tell you the truth, anyone who believes in
me, will have eternal life. (John 1:47)

The psalmist wrote in Psalm 37:23 that, "the steps of a good man are ordered by the Lord." We have a set of guidelines for when we are angry and anxious with circumstances and people in our lives. David wrote in Psalm 37:

Do not be agitated by evil doers or envy
those who do wrong.

Trust in the Lord and take delight in the Lord and commit your way to Him. Paul tell us in the fourth chapter of Philippians to not worry about anything, but in everything, give thanks to the Lord and present your requests to Him. God's Word is the only true navigation system for our lives. His word provides direction, and when we turn the wrong way, His spirit gently recalculates us in the right direction.

> If we confess our sins, He is faithful and just
> to forgive us our sins and to cleanse us from all
> unrighteousness. (1 John 1:9)

His Word directs us to confess and repent. The Lord will recalculate us as many times needed. Everything we need is in His word. Timothy wrote in chapter 3, verse 16:

> All scripture is given by inspiration of God
> and is profitable for doctrine, for reproof, for cor-
> rection, for instruction in righteousness that the
> man of God shall be complete and thoroughly
> equipped for every good work.

Life has many ups, downs, curves, and sharp turns, so plug in to the navigation system that always works!

Cloud of Reflection

Write Proverbs 3:6 on an index card and place where you can read it each day.

Hit the Pause Button

For Your steadfast loves is great above the
heavens, Your faithfulness reaches to the
clouds. Be exalted O God, above the heavens!
Let Your glory be all over the earth!

—Psalm 108:4–5

The alarm goes off, and our day takes off to the races. The hours are filled with job duties, appointments, and events. Depending on the season of life you are in, the days may be filled with job meetings with coworkers or perhaps you are retired, and your days are tee times and lunch dates with friends. Regardless of what season you are in, the days fly by like the wind.

There are days when the alarm does not go off, the washer is not working, you are late for an appointment because you are stuck in traffic, and then a child calls with a problem. Can anyone besides me relate? That's when I want to say, "Hit the pause button. I need to catch my breath!"

God's Word tells us to *hit the pause button* in Psalm 46:10:

Be still and know that I am God.

In the midst of the chaos, it is difficult to pause, to be still, but this is exactly what God wants His children to do.

In 1 Kings 19:11–12, we have the account of Elijah at Mount Horeb. The previous verses inform us of how he fled from wicked Jezebel and was done. Elijah cried to God, "It is enough!" The Lord instructs Elijah to rest and eat. In verses eleven and twelve, God told

Elijah to stop and stand on the mountain before Him. The Lord brought a mighty wind, but He was not in it. He then created an earthquake, and the ground shook, but He was not in it. And then the earthquake was followed by a fire, still the Lord was not there! Then after the fire, there was a small still voice, and the Lord was there! It was not until Elijah hit the pause button and stopped that He could hear the Lord. The same is true for us when the storms of life hit us. While the winds are raging and the earth is shaking, stop and listen for God.

> In returning and rest you shall be saved;
> in quietness and in trust shall be your strength.
> (Isaiah 30:15)

What is the Lord wanting you to hear today? Hit the pause button and listen for His small still voice.

> The Lord God is in your midst, a mighty one who will save; He will rejoice over you with gladness; He will quiet you with His love.
> (Zephaniah 3:5)

Cloud of Reflection

Memorize Psalm 46:10.

Holes in the Cake

Create in me a clean heart, O God.
Renew a loyal spirit within me.

—Psalm 51:10 (NLT)

Everyone loves a good pound cake. I have a recipe that is simple and delicious. At the time of writing this, I have probably baked over two hundred cakes. Of course, by now I have the recipe memorized and hardly think of the steps until recently. I baked a cake for a party, and it looked perfect on the outside; however, when slicing it, there were large holes in all the slices. I was horrified and decided that the eggs must be old, so I went to store and bought new eggs and baked cake number two. And I couldn't believe my eyes when I cut into cake number two. It, too, was full of holes. I went to Google to find out what was causing holes in my cakes. Wise Google stated that usually it was a result over mixing. I changed my mixing method, and alas cake number three was hole-free!

The other cakes looked perfect with all the right ingredients; however, air bubbles had creeped inside, resulting in holes. Our lives can be similar to my cake. On the outside, everything looks perfect with all the right pieces; however, on the inside is a different story. Tiny air bubbles of bitterness, jealousy, anger, and discontentment creep into our hearts resulting in holes. These holes rob us of joy, strength, and peace.

A sound heart is life to the body, but envy is
rottenness to the bones. (Proverbs 14:30)

And also in book of Proverbs 4:23:

Guard your heart above all else, for it deter-
mines the course of your life.

We must pay attention to our heart condition and discard those small thoughts of bitterness, envy, and discontentment. The psalmist asked the Lord in Psalm 139:23–24 to search his heart:

> Search me, O God, and know my heart, Try me and know my anxieties and see if there is any wicked way in me, And lead me in the way everlasting.

Paul provides us with an outline in Philippians 4:8–9:

> "Finally brethren, whatever things are true, whatever are noble, whatever things are just, whatever things are pure, whatever is lovely and whatever is of good report; if there is any virtue and if there is anything praiseworthy, meditate on these things. And the peace of God will be with you."

This is how Paul learned to be content and not let bitterness and anger destroy his heart in the midst of his trails and persecution. Follow God's recipe for a healthy heart free of holes.

> And let the peace that comes from Christ rule in your hearts. (Colossians 3:15)

Cloud of Reflection

Write down any areas in your life that can result in holes in your heart. Write a prayer asking God to remove them.

Home Sweet Home

Abide in Me and I in you.

—John 15:4

Home sweet home—a place of security and comfort. When we are in our homes, there is a sense of belonging. There is no reason to dress up and attempt to impress someone. We are at home and can just be ourselves. The dictionary's definition is a permanent place of living. A lot of time, money, and energy are spent in creating the perfect place we call home. We spend hours finding the right decorations to make it sparkle and personal. Home is our starting and ending point. We start and end our day here. Regardless of the kind of day we have had, home is the place we can relax and rest. Even after a spectacular vacation, it always good to come home. Home is where the heart is.

Our earthly homes, however, are only temporary. As children of the King, we have a home that will not perish. Our Father has a place with many rooms. We never have to worry about a No Vacancy sign being posted.

As we walk through this journey on earth, Jesus tells us to abide in Him. We have our earthly houses built by man, but the One who has built everything is God (Hebrews 3:4).

Jesus tells us in John 15:10 how to abide in Him:

If you keep my commandments, you will abide in My love.

And His commandment is stated clearly and simply in verse twelve:

> This is my commandment that you love
> one another as I have loved you.

Abiding in our Lord God results in peace and love. Imagine how different our earthly homes would be if we abided in Christ. The prophet Isaiah in chapter 32, verses 16–20 talks about the peace of God's reign. The work of righteousness is peace. Verse 18 (NKJV):

> My people will dwell in a peaceful habi-
> tation, in secure dwellings and in quiet resting
> places.

Without abiding in Christ, we can accomplish nothing. If we abide in Him and His words live through us, whatever we ask shall be done for His glory.

A fulfilling lasting home sweet home is abiding with our Lord. God's Word says to love one another as he has loved you. It does not say love those whom you love or care about. Jesus calls us to love those who hurt us, do not deserve our love, have different lifestyles, and those who are unlovable. "Abide in My love then and only then can you truly love."

Cloud of
Reflection

Write down someone or a group of people that you need to love. Pray for God to show you how to love them.

Hopeful Living in a Hopeless World

> But hope that is seen is not hope. But
> if we hope for what we do not see, we
> eagerly wait for it with perseverance.
>
> —Romans 8:24–25

The fact we live in a hopeless world is not breaking news. The media reports one catastrophic event after another: school shootings, wild fires, floods, volcanoes erupting, and earthquakes to name on a few. So are we to be hopeful in this chaotic and fallen world? Being the visual people we are, we look for hope, thinking if we find it, all will be right. But hope is something that is not seen.

In the gospel of Luke 18:35–43 is the story of a blind man. In the ancient days, beggars were shunned by society, unable to get jobs and take care of themselves. They would walk along roads filled with people, begging for money. In this situation, the blind man was sitting by the road and heard the crowd and asked what was going on. The people told him that Jesus of Nazareth was passing by. So guess what the blind man did next? He began to cry out.

"Son of David, have mercy on me!" The people around him told him to be quiet, and the more they told him to be quiet, the louder he became. The blind man could not see Jesus, but he had hope in the power of the Son of David.

Jesus heard the blind man and had him brought to him and asked, "What do you want from me?" The blind man did not stop to think but quickly responded that he wanted his sight. Then Jesus said to him, "Receive your sight. Your faith has made you well." The blind man had hope in what he could not see. Faith that is seen is not faith.

The only hope we have for ourselves is to give up hope in ourselves. Put our hope in the Lord God who is able to do all things. Nothing is impossible for God! Perhaps today you feel hopeless, and the circumstances you are facing seems impossible. Hopelessness constricts and withers the heart, rendering it unable to sense God's blessing and grace. When we are hopeless, we exaggerate the adversities of life, making us feel the burden is too great to bear. Romans 4: 18–19 mentions Abraham:

> In hope he believed against hope, that he
> should become the father of many nations.

The blind man could not see but had faith in what he could not see—the power of Jesus! Whatever mountain is in front of you today, take your eyes off of it and trust in the power of Jesus.

> Now faith is the assurance of things hoped for,
> the conviction of things not seen. (Hebrews 11:1)

A quote by evangelist Jay Lowder:

> A miracle will not bring me faith but my
> faith can bring a miracle.

Cloud of Reflection

Memorize Hebrews 11:1.

In a Moment...
Everything Changed

Listen, I tell you a mystery. We will not all
sleep, but we will all be changed in a flash, in
the twinkling of an eye, at the last trumpet.
For the trumpet will sound, the dead will be
raised imperishable and we will be changed.

—1 Corinthians 15:51–52

Life is a perpetual motion similar to the ebb and flow of the ocean.
When I sit on the beach, I am mesmerized by the constant rush of
the waves pounding the shore. As the waves hit the shore, shells and
sand are washed in and out and rearranged. Our journey on this road
of life is impacted daily with changes, some gradual while others are
drastic and sudden. One day you wake up and the arms and legs that
were once firm and strong are now covered with crepe-like skin and
flabby. When did that happen? Only a short time ago you were rocking your children and now you are rocking theirs.

Unfortunately, some changes are catastrophic and unexpected—a diagnosis of cancer, unexpected financial crisis, a loss of a
loved one to just name a few. These events leave us overwhelmed and
scrambling for solutions like the shells on the sand when the waves
hit.

In John 14:1–2 Jesus tells us:

> Let not your heart be troubled; believe in
> God. In my Father's house there are many rooms
> and I go to prepare a place for you.

In this world, we will have trials and difficulties, but the author of Hebrews tells us that we have a high priest who understands and sympathizes with us. As children of God, we can come boldly to the throne of grace where we find mercy, love, and grace. Paul writes in 2 Corinthians 12:9:

> My grace is sufficient for you, for my power
> is made perfect in weakness.

A few weeks ago, I stood at my sweet mother's bedside, watching her drift from this earthly home to her heavenly one. For several days, she declined, and each breath was a struggle. And then suddenly, in a moment, everything changed, and my mother was with her Savior. In a moment, everything changed not only for her but for me. The one who raised me, supported me, and taught me how to be a prayer warrior was no longer with me. As difficult as that is, I have peace because I know that she is healed and in heaven with her Lord.

Just as with Jesus. Three days after all the horror and pain and suffering on the cross, in a moment everything changed! He arose out of the grave, and death lost its sting. No death, no more tears, ours is the victory! And Jesus gave us the Holy Spirit to guide and comfort us.

> He will wipe away every tear from their eyes,
> and death shall be no more; neither shall there
> be mourning nor crying, nor pain anymore; for
> the former things have passed away. (Revelation
> 21:4)

In a moment, yes, everything changed. Praise the Lord we have a Savior who is always with us. He will rescue and save us, and one day, in a moment, we will be walking in the rooms of His mansion, which He prepared for us!

> But take heart, I have overcome the world.
> (John 16:13)

We are overcomers through belief in Jesus Christ and have everlasting life. Praise God!

Cloud of Reflection

Spend time reflecting what it means to you that Jesus has overcome the world. Journal your thoughts.

In This Mountain

And in this mountain, The Lord of hosts
will make for all people a feast."

—Isaiah 25:6

There is a significant difference between being on top of the mountain or in the middle of it. When we are on top of the mountain, we have no fear. We are confident and powerful, and nothing can shake us. However, in the mountain, up against it, we are overwhelmed. All we see is the height of the mountain looming over us. And fear descends upon us, leaving us powerless.

Is there a mountain in your life that you are up against? A situation that seems impossible to climb above? Those mountains come into our lives in a variety of forms. Prodigal children, broken marriages, financial failures are just a few. So how do we get to the top of that mountain, the impossible situation? David faced impossible mountains in his life, and he knew where to turn to get to the top. He tells us in Psalm 121:1–2:

I will lift up my eyes to the hills, From where
does my help come from? My help comes from
the Lord, who made heaven and earth.

When we are faced with the impossible, we are to look up to the Creator of this universe. When our focus is on the mountain, it is stops us moving forward. In this mountain, God is working for our good.

For I know the plans I have for you, declares
the Lord, plans for welfare and not for evil, to
give you a future and a hope. (Jeremiah 29:11)

God's ways are not our ways, but we must trust that His way is always the right way.

In this passage Isaiah 25:6–8, God has the prophet tell the people that in this mountain, He will make a feast for all people—a feast of food—and He will swallow up this mountain and wipe away all tears. God promises the children of Israel freedom from their mountain of bondage. God's promise to us today is the same. In this situation we are facing, our Lord God is working. Yahweh, our eternal God, is working. Trust in Him and seek His presence.

I cried aloud to the Lord and he answered
me from His holy hill. (Psalm 3:4)

Remember when you are against the mountain that God is present and He will prepare a feast—good things—and He will wipe away your tears. Look up and praise Him for what He will do.

*Cloud of
Reflection*

Write a prayer of praise, thanking God for His presence in your mountain.

It Just Snaps Together

But seek first the kingdom of God
and His righteousness and all these
things will be added to you.

—Matthew 6:33

We recently moved to a new house with a large outdoor kitchen and pool area, and that of course, required new furniture. I spent hours shopping for the perfect patio furniture with a great price. I finally found everything online with awesome prices with one little obstacle: the furniture required assembly. While I was excited about the purchases, my husband did not share the same excitement with the task of assembling the furniture. My response to him was, "It just snaps together!" Needless to say, the furniture required more than snapping together. It required reading and following the instructions and using the proper tools.

Wouldn't it be wonderful if our daily lives just snapped together? Different seasons in our lives are often challenging and difficult to assemble. Raising our children, careers, finances, and health issues do not just snap together the way we want. So what do we do when our lives do not go together the way we planned? Read the instructions and follow them. God's Word provides us with the instructions to put our lives together according to His will—instructions for our Christian walk, raising our children, and our jobs. To assemble our lives correctly, we must read the instructions and have the proper tools. God's Word is the proper tool.

Trust in the Lord with all your heart and do
not lean on your own understanding. In all your
ways acknowledge him and he will make straight
your paths. (Proverbs 3: 5–6)

Snap together lives would be great, but that is not the way God
has designed it. Only when we read the instructions and follow them
does it go to together, and He receives the glory. He wants us to seek
Him, read His Word, and follow His instructions.

All scriptures is breathed out by God and
profitable for teaching, for reproof, for correction
and for training in righteousness, that the man of
God be complete and equipped for every good
work. (2 Timothy 3:16)

Cloud of
Reflection

Reflect on an area in your life that want to just snap together.

Find a verse that instructs you in this area

It's All about Grace

And He said to me: "My grace is sufficient for
you; My strength is made perfect in weakness."

—2 Corinthians 12:9

We live in an "It's All about Me" society. Social media promotes this mentality that everything has to be "all about me." People post their moods, conflicts, happy events, disasters, and yes, even their food on Facebook and Instagram. Conflicts in our relationships in the family or work environment is the product of it's-all-about-Me mentality. Can you imagine a government that is not controlled by politicians with the all-about-me mentality? How different would our relationships in our homes, churches, and work be if our decisions and choices were not based on our agendas and opinion.

One day I was asking Siri on my iPhone a simple question regarding converting teaspoons in a recipe. Every time I asked, her she would reply with a comment that had nothing to do with the question. I became frustrated and said, "Siri, you are not listening and making this difficult."

Her response was, "It's not all about you, Janmarie!" Really? Did Siri not understand that it was truly all about me!

Our personal relationship with Christ can be reflective of the all-about-me mentality. We pray when our world crashes, and spending time in God's word is sandwiched in between our moods and activities. How bless we are to have a God who is all about grace! Grace is defined as God's favor toward the unworthy and undeserving. In His grace, God is willing to forgive us and bless us in spite of our failures and weaknesses. All of us are born in sin and unable to keep God's laws.

Paul wrote in the second chapter of Ephesians that we are saved by grace.

> For you are saved by grace through faith—
> and this is not from yourselves, it is the gift of
> God—not by works, so that no one can boast.
> (Ephesians 2:8–9 NIV).

In John 1:16:

> And of His fullness we have all received, and
> grace for grace.

One translation is grace upon grace implying a constant overflowing gift. We have a God who continually gives us grace in a world where there is no grace. When we face mountains that won't move or storms that don't pass over, there is God's abounding grace. Paul knew this grace when he asked the Lord to remove a thorn in his flesh, not once but three times. And the Lord's response was, "My grace is sufficient for you. My strength is made perfect in weakness."

Maybe today you are facing a mountain or a storm, and you are unsure how to go on. Trust the One who created the mountains and storms. He knows the way around the mountain and through the storm clouds. And until then, while you are waiting, His grace is all you need.

> And God is able to make every grace over-
> flow to you, so that in every way always have
> everything you need, you may excel in every
> good work. (2 Corinthians 9:8)

Amazing grace, how sweet the sound. Yes, it truly is Amazing grace!

Cloud of
Reflection

What area in your life do you need to allow God's grace to be enough while you are waiting for Him to lead you? Write it down and then write a prayer asking the Lord to help.

Law and Order

Everyone must submit himself to the
governing authorities for there is not authority
except that which God has established.

—Romans 13:1 (NIV)

One of the most viewed television series is *Law and Order*. Millions watch this drama series of determining guilt or innocence of people caught up in ethical personal and legal dilemmas. The episodes are frequently adapted from our current headlines. Law and order is essential in order to survive in our world today. The laws in our country protect us from living in a constant state of chaos. In a free society, every man lives under a rule of law as opposed to an eccentric rule of man. A rule of law is to protect the individual and is a guideline for minimally acceptable behavior in society.

While it is true that we want to live in an orderly environment, there are certain rules and laws that we don't agree with or think necessary. One illustration of this is the prohibition of cell phone use when driving. Most Americans think this means most of the time and nothing will happen with one text or call, and besides, its important. That is exactly what a young man told the authorities when he crashed head on into a church bus, killing thirteen senior adults while he was texting. What a tragic consequence to not adhering to a simple law.

Paul instructed the church in Rome in chapter 13, verses 1–5 to submit to the government authorities. Verse two states, "consequently he who rebels against the authority is rebelling against what God has instituted." In our present day, it is difficult to see and believe that some of our leaders are instituted by God. We can rationalize that there are laws that conflict with God's laws. However, God's Word is clear that we are to follow the laws of the government. We are never to submit to laws that are directly disobedient to God's commands. The laws of the land relate to our physical being, and the laws of God relate to our spiritual being. Peter tells the Christians in 1 Peter 2:13–16 to submit for the Lord's sake to every authority among men whether to the king or to the governor. Peter was not saying to compromise their faith to God but to live according to the laws of the land as responsible citizens. The religious leaders attempted to trap Jesus by asking if it was right to pay taxes to Caesar and His reply was, "Give to Caesar what is his and to God what belongs to God." (Luke 20:25)

Our God wants us to be an example of a responsible citizen. This requires not only following the laws but praying for our authorities. We find it easy to pray for our needs and those we care about, but how often do we pray for our leaders? Our responsibility is not to judge, criticize or disrespect our leaders but to pray for their leadership and spiritual condition.

> Remind the believers to submit to the government and its officers. They should be obedient always ready to do what is good. (Titus 3:1)

Cloud of Reflection

Designate a day of the week to pray for our national, state, and local leaders. Write a prayer asking the Lord to give them wisdom.

Life is not Always a Straight Line

The steps of a man are established by the
Lord, when he delights in his way; though
he fall, he shall not be cast headlong,
for the Lord upholds his hand.

—Psalm 37:23–24

We learned at an early age how to color in a straight line and that our artwork needs to be neat and in straight lines. For some of us, drawing a straight line is a challenge in which a ruler is essential.

Not only do we want our artwork in a straight line, but we also want our life in a straight line, without any wrinkles or bumps. We graduate from college with plans for our careers, get married, and buy our dream home and have a family. With all these events, we want them smooth and wrinkle-free. With a straight-line life, there is contentment and joy; however, what happens when life is not a straight line and the way is full of wrinkles and obstacles? Our lives oftentimes is not as we planned it. Children rebel, jobs end, finances crumble, and health fails. During these times, we may be unsure which direction to go; however, as children of the King, we have a ruler to straighten the crooked lines in our life. If our lives were always a straight line, we would not use our ruler. When life happens, this is the time God works in our life doing what only God can do.

In Isaiah 43:19:

> Behold, I will do a new thing, now it shall spring forth, shall you not know it? I will even make a road in the wilderness, And rivers in the desert.

The prophet Isaiah instructs us in chapter 41, verse 10 to "fear not, for I am with you; be not dismayed, for I am your God; I will strengthen you, I will help you, I will uphold you with My righteous right hand."

Yes, it would be great if our lives were always in a straight line, free of obstacles and wrinkles, but that is not God's plan.

> For I know the plans I have for you, declares the Lord, plans for welfare and not for evil, to give you a future and a hope. (Jeremiah 29:11)

God's Word doesn't say your plans or agendas. It says His plans, and his way is perfect. Perhaps your life is crooked today, turn to the ruler of the universe, our creator and master designer.

> When my heart is overwhelmed, lead me to the rock that is higher than I. (Psalm 61:2)

Cloud of Reflection

Memorize Jeremiah 29:11 and remind yourself when your plans don't work out, that the creator of the universe has it in control.

Life is Simple

The Lord is my Shepherd, I have all that I need.

—Psalm 23:1

When you reflect on the world we live in, it is anything but simple. Our jobs are filled with regulations and challenges. Our children have their lives packed with a variety of activities, and daily decisions regarding finances, health, and careers are often complicated. While technology simplifies life to an extent, it often times also creates more chaos. A seemingly simple decision to take a vacation involves making decisions regarding location, transportation, lodging, activities, and don't forget the price! Relationships with families and others can be complicated due to differences in opinions.

King David states in the twenty-third chapter of Psalms that life is simple because the Lord is our shepherd and we have everything we need. Jesus gave us a model prayer found in Matthew 6:9:

Our Father who is in heaven, hallowed be
your name.

How simple our life would be if we acknowledge daily Our Father in heaven and hallowed His name. Hallowed is referring to the holiness of God. When we pray, we acknowledge that God is holy. How different would your life be if you acknowledge God's holiness in your quiet time, agendas, jobs, finances, and relationships? Acknowledging His holiness guides us to be like Him.

1 Peter 1:15–16:

> But now you must be holy in everything
> you do, just as God who calls you is holy. For the
> scripture says, "You must be holy for I am holy."

You are probably thinking how can I possibly be holy? We will never achieve true holiness, but we are to work toward that goal. Paul presents a strategy in Colossians chapter 3 to assist us to live for God. Verse 12 instructs us to clothe ourselves with compassion, kindness, humility, gentleness, and patience.

In verse 13:

> Bear with each other and forgive whatever
> grievances you have against one another. Forgive
> as the Lord forgives you.

Let love guide your actions and be thankful. Spend time in the presence of our Heavenly Father praying and reading His word.

This world of ours will never be simple, but a personal relationship with Jesus is simple. His ways are simple and perfect.

> In all your ways acknowledge Him and He
> will make your paths straight. (Proverbs 3:6)

Cloud of
Reflection

Reflect on God's simple love for you. Write a verse that reminds you to live life simply.

Lift Ticket

Humble yourselves in the sight of the
Lord and He will lift you up.

—James 4:10

Snow skiing is one of the most popular winter sports. Resorts cater to visitors, making trails clean and clear, trail maps for directions, and lodging and food accommodations. Resorts provide ski schools for beginners starting as early as three years old. Our family goes skiing every year. Preparation for this trip starts with scheduling transportation and finding a place to stay. After arrival, the process of renting ski equipment and purchasing lift tickets begins. Lift tickets are required for everyday that one skis and must stay in your pocket at all times in order to get on the lift to go to top of mountain.

As children of God, we, too, have a lift ticket to the top of the mountain. We don't have to purchase our ticket; it is free and our Lord Jesus purchased it for us.

For God so loved the world that He gave
His only begotten son, that whoever believes in
Him shall not perish but have everlasting life.
(John 3:16)

We have done nothing to earn this ticket for everlasting life.

For by grace you have been saved through
faith, and not that of yourselves; it is the gift of
God. (Ephesians 2:8)

Our journey to the top of the mountain is oftentimes rocky, and the path is uneven. However, we have a trail map, God's Word, to guide and direct us. Our key verse tells us how to be lifted up. We are to humble ourselves in His presence. The requirement to be lifted up does not requires a lift ticket but for us to humble ourselves and trust Our Lord God. The definition of humble is to have a modest estimate of one's self being without arrogance. A humble person does not think he is better than someone else. When we humble ourselves to Our Creator, we acknowledge that we have no power of our own and not worth of His love. Worry and seeking man's interventions to fix our circumstances exhibits a lack of trust in God's power.

Your trail may have rocks of depression, loneliness, illness or heartbreak, and you are unsure of the direction you need to go. In Chapter 121 of Psalms, David writes of where his strength comes from:

> I will lift my eyes toward the mountains;
> Where does my help come from? My help comes
> from the Lord, the maker of heaven and earth.

David was afraid and distraught when he was fleeing for Absalom and wrote:

> But You, O Lord, are a shield for me, my
> glory and the One who lifts me up. (Psalm 3:3)

We have the ultimate everlasting lift ticket, Jesus Christ Our Savior, and His way is perfect, and He is always faithful.

Cloud of Reflection

Memorize Psalm 121.

Looking for Happiness in All the Wrong Places

> For my people have done two evil things:
> They have abandoned me-the fountain of
> living water. And they have dug for themselves
> cracked cisterns that can hold no water at all!
>
> —Jeremiah 2:13 (NLT)

A cistern was an artificial reservoir, which was dug in the earth or carved in the rock to store water in the ancient Bible days. Cisterns were essential for survival due to long dry seasons and scarce springs. A broken cistern was useless; crumbling stone could hold only a small amount of water or none at all. It would be like us putting air in a tire without the plug in. The message from Jeremiah in chapter 2 was to get the attention of the people of Judah to see their foolish ways. They had turned from the fountain of living water and were looking elsewhere to quench their thirst. The children of Israel dug cisterns of idolatry and immorality, thinking the human pleasures would satisfy. But what they discovered is that their cisterns were cracked and could not hold water. These cisterns were broken from the start and not damaged later. The same is true for us today. Cisterns of our own making to find contentment and happiness that is not in line with God's truth will always result in failure and heartbreak.

The prophet Isaiah in chapter 55, verses 1–2 tells the people, "Come everyone who is thirsty, come to the waters; and you have no money, come, buy and eat! Come, buy wine and milk without money and without cost. Why spend money on what is not bread, and your labor on what does not satisfy? Listen, listen to me, and eat what is good, and you will delight in the riches of fare."

Our Lord God provides us with everlasting nourishment. All the things of this world we search for is temporary; our possessions and wealth cannot provide contentment that lasts. The key scripture reflects that the people of Judah committed two wrongs. One was to construct an artificial reservoir for spiritual water; however, the second was more tragic. The people rejected the fountain of life. We may ask ourselves who in their right mind would turn away from a sparkling fountain of fresh water to a vessel that is cracked and unable to hold water. However, are we any different than the people of Judah? We can easily become indifferent to the fountain of living water and wander away making our own cisterns. We search for contentment and peace in cisterns of money, power, material possessions, and relationships for a few examples. Ask yourself, Where do you spend the most of your time and money? What does your entertainment list look like? There is nothing wrong with travel, movies, sporting events or money unless it is our focus.

Another common cistern today is social media. How easy it is to become consumed with happenings on Facebook, Instagram and Twitter and lose sight of what is important. Our first priority daily should be to spend time with our Lord and not to pick up our phone to search for the latest events on social media. Can anyone relate to this besides me? In the Gospel of John chapter 6, verse 35, it says, "I am the bread of life. No one who comes to me will ever be hungry and no one who believes in me will never be thirsty again." This is everlasting nourishment, and regardless of the state of your life, the fountain of Jesus's love and peace is the answer. Choose this day a cistern that is strong and leak-proof.

Seek the kingdom of God above all else and
live righteously and He will give you everything
you need. (Matthew 6:33 NLT)

Cloud of
Reflection

What areas in your life are cracked cisterns? Write them down and ask the Lord to heal

Losing the Connection

But Your steadfast love is great
and above the heavens and Your
faithfulness reaches to the clouds.

—Psalm 108:4

The busy complex twenty-first century we live in is all about being connected. We connect to social media and the internet so we can be informed of the events happening around us and in this world. Our Smart TV connects us to a variety of entertainment. A few weeks ago, lightning struck an AT&T tower resulting in large areas of our state being without service. We were unable to view TV, check the internet or even use our apps on our phones because of no Wi-Fi. We had no information regarding the weather status, the government or the drama of Facebook. For most of the day, my husband and I were lost and not sure what we could do. Finally later in the day, we got out the Monopoly board. Whatever happened to those days? Technology happened, and we are unable to go through a day without checking the internet or our social media accounts.

We experience the same feeling of being lost and not knowing what direction to take when we are going through difficult times. At times, our world feels secure and connected, and then out of the sky is a power outage. A critical health issue, a broken relationship, a natural disaster that wipes away everything you have worked for are just a few examples of power outages in our life. During this time, it is difficult to know what to do or where to go. And perhaps during this time, you feel disconnected from our Lord Jesus Christ. His word assures us that there is no power outage with Him.

> For I am persuaded that neither death no
> life, nor angels, nor principalities, nor powers,
> nor things present nor things to come, nor height
> nor depth, nor any other created thing, shall sep-
> arate us from the love of God, which is in Christ
> Jesus our Lord. (Romans 8:38–39)

What an amazing promise we have that we cannot experience a power outage from Our God. We may not feel any power, but when we plug into His presence, He will give us all the power that we need to get through this time.

Psalm 142:3:

> When my spirit was overwhelmed within
> me, Then you knew my path.

We have an everlasting connection to the One who is able to do all things.

> Do not be afraid, nor be dismayed, for the
> Lord Your God is with you wherever you go.
> (Joshua 1:9)

Connect with the power that never has an outage.

Cloud of Reflection

Write a verse that reminds you of the everlasting power of God

Mud Puddles

The mind of sinful man is death, the mind
controlled by the Spirit is life and peace.

—Romans 8:6

I have never figured out the attraction between children and puppies to mud puddles. The puddles are like magnets luring them to get right in the middle regardless of how much you attempt to detour them, and in spite of all the stern warnings, the temptation is too great to resist. It never fails that right after our schnauzer, Dixie, is groomed that it rains. And in spite of all my warnings and detours, she is still manages to get right in the middle of a mud puddle. At that moment, she is happy and jumping around; however, she is not so happy about the cleaning up process.

We, too, are attracted to mud puddles in our life. We hear the warning and see the detour signs but keep on until we are right in the middle of the mud puddle. Mud puddles of gossip, greed, pride, and hatred draw us like magnets. Our desires for wealth, power, and fame pull us into the puddle. And then we realize that we are stained and need to be cleaned up. God instructs us in His word:

You shall walk in all the ways of the Lord your
God has commanded you; that you may live and
that it may be well with you. (Deuteronomy 5:33)

The first step in the clean up process is to recognize that we have sinned.

For all have sinned and fall short of the
glory of God. (Romans 3:23)

David in Psalm 32:5 DECLARES, "I will confess my transgressions to the Lord." The only way out of the mud puddle is through the power of Jesus Christ. Only when we seek His presence and desire to change, can we be free of the stain. Hatred, pride, envy and anger destroy God's joy and peace in our life.

> Now the works of the flesh are evident which are adultery, uncleanness, anger selfishness. (Galatians 5:19)

And verse twenty-two says, "But the fruits of the spirit is love, joy and peace."

Mud puddles will always be in our lives; however, we have a power greater than that of the world.

> For we do not have a high priest who cannot sympathize with our weaknesses, but in all points tempted as we are, yet without sin. Let us therefore come boldly to the throne of grace that we may obtain mercy and find grace to help us in our time of need. (Hebrews 4:13–14)

Turn to Lord Jesus to clean and free you from your mud puddle.

Cloud of Reflection

What mud puddles pull you in? Write a prayer asking the Lord to give you strength to be free of them.

On the Road of Life

The heart of man plans his way, but
the Lord establishes his steps.

—Proverbs 16:9

Traveling is one of my favorite things to do regardless if it is by car, plane or air. Planning the trip is sometimes the most fun. We check travel times, hotels reservations, and attractions and things to do when we get to our destination. For those of you who have traveled frequently, you understand that oftentimes, our perfectly planned itineraries do not always work out the way we planned.

The same is true for this journey of life. We spend countless hours and energy planning our itinerary and our children. During this time of Mother's Day, I'm reminded that just as travel itineraries change, the same is true with our children. The itinerary I have planned is not how their life is turning out. My personal journey of motherhood has been happy and sad, smooth and rough and hopeful and disappointing. And yes, I would not change anything for this journey.

As children of the King, Our heavenly Father, too, has the perfect itinerary for us and our children. While we may think our plan is the best, Our Father knows what the best is.

For I know the plans I have for you, declares
the Lord, plans for welfare and not for evil, to
give you a future and a hope. (Jeremiah 28:11)

The way to have a successful itinerary is to commit your way to the Lord. Stop trying to find ways to make it perfect and allow our Lord to work it for His glory. His unfailing, unconditional love will guide us on this journey. Life is not a destination but a journey. Regardless if the road has bumps or is smooth, The Master has the plan, and His grace is sufficient.

Cloud of Reflection

Write on post it note 2 Corinthians 12:9.

Pass Interference

Trust in the Lord with all your heart and do
not depend on your own understanding.

—Proverbs 3:5

Football, one of Americans' most popular sports, is woven into our society. Children start in grade school playing this physical sport, which began in England over a hundred years ago. Our high schools focus their energy and activities around the success of their football program.

A popular movie several years ago entitled *Friday Night Lights* is a story about the completion and drama of high school football in Texas. Colleges spend major money and time in recruitment to make a name for themselves. Americans not only spend time and money watching NFL but also spend lots of energy on playing Fantasy Football. There are events in the game that can suddenly change the direction of the game such as a touchdown, penalties, interceptions or pass interference calls. Pass interference occurs when a player interferes with an eligible receiver's ability to make a catch resulting in a penalty that often result in a setback.

Pass interference occurs in our lives too. Most of the time, we never see it coming, and it brings our current direction to a halt. Interruptions and interference are something our human nature has no patience for. Some interferences are minor such as electricity off for a short time, a severe thunderstorm or a short illness such as flu. However, other interferences can be life-changing events that totally change our direction—signing divorce paper instead of celebrating an anniversary, planning a funeral instead of a vacation, job hunting instead of a promotion, visiting a child in prison instead of college or rummaging through the remains of your house after a natural disaster instead of remodeling.

Our forward progress stops, and we are unsure what steps to take next. Change involves adapting and moving to something unfamiliar. An illustration of this is found in the book of Ruth, which begins with Naomi and her husband leaving their village to live in Moab due to the famine. Later her husband dies, and her two sons marry, but then another interference: both of her sons die, leaving her with two daughters-in-law. They travel back to Bethlehem, and Naomi tries to get Ruth to leave and go back to her own people, but Ruth refuses. She didn't choose Naomi, but the God of Israel.

This should be the same for us during life-changing interruptions. We are not to choose the situation but to choose to trust God and His plan. God allows interferences to draw us out of our comfort zone to rely on His strength and not our own. Our faith grows and becomes stronger when we are outside our comfort zone. We see in Ruth's situation how God provided her Boaz, and she gave birth to Obed and the beginnings of the lineage of David. Out of death and famine, God brought fulfillment and a future. The story of Ruth shows us how the most difficult interferences can be God's provision for our life.

> For my thoughts and your ways are not my
> ways; declares the Lord. (Isaiah 55:8)

Maybe today you are facing a difficult situation and interference that has change your life direction. Be encouraged. God is faithful. Trust Him in spite of the difficulty. In chapter 43 of Isaiah verse 19, it states, "For I am about to do something new, See I have already begun! Do you not see it? I will make a pathway in the wilderness. I will create rivers in the dry wasteland."

Cloud of
Reflection

Reflect on an interference in your life and journal how God brought you out of it. Write a verse of His faithfulness.

Priceless

Anyone trusting in his riches will fall but
the righteous will flourish like foliage.

—Proverbs 11:28

Price tags! Everywhere we look there is a price tag on items we want or think we need. We especially like those price tags that have been reduced. Price tags mark the value of what we want to buy such as groceries, clothes, houses to name a few items. Most of us are familiar with the Mastercard slogan, "Some things money cannot buy, but for everything else, there is Mastercard." This slogan was started in 1997, targeting experiences that are valuable and money cannot buy such as VIP tickets to a World Series game. The experience is priceless, but Mastercard can purchase it.

We research and review price tags for all types of items; however, we fail to evaluate the price tags for a futile life filled with worldly things. Riches cannot last or satisfy. Solomon wrote in the second chapter of Ecclesiastes how he built houses and planted gardens and acquired gold and large herds and enjoyed any pleasure he wanted. Then he evaluated his achievement and found it to be futile and a pursuit of the wind. God tells us to seek heavenly treasures, not the earthly treasures that perish.

The story of the rich young ruler illustrates how material wealth can separate us for spiritual growth and a personal relationship with Jesus Christ. This is one of the few passages that deals directly with wealth and is found in the Gospel of Matthew chapter 19, verses 16–22 as well as in the Gospels of Mark and Luke.

The rich young ruler was a prince, probably a ruler in the Jewish synagogue. He inquired of Jesus, "What good thing shall I do to have eternal life?" Jesus told him to keep all the commandments, and the young ruler responded that he had done all that. Then he asked Jesus, "What do I lack?" This is a key statement demonstrating that he knew that his riches were not enough, and he was incomplete spiritually.

Jesus instructs him to sell his possessions to the poor and follow Him and seek heavenly treasures. The young man was greatly saddened and walked away. The issue was not that he had wealth, instead, the wealth was his idol, a substitute for God. His attachment to his riches controlled his willingness to obey Jesus. He failed to follow the commandment to love the Lord your God with all your heart. Riches and earthly treasures are not wrong unless we place them ahead of our Lord God. We live in a world focused on possessions and instant gratification; however, none of these can satisfy.

> The one who loves silver is never satisfied with silver and whoever loves wealth is never satisfied with income. (Ecclesiastes 5:20)

Having a love for anything or person greater that our love for God is an idol and will only destroy us. We are warned about money in 1 Timothy 6:10:

> For the love of money is the root of all evil.

What possessions possess you? Does your checkbook reflect that you love the Lord your God with all your heart? The young ruler had money for anything he wanted; however, for a relationship with Jesus—priceless and something money cannot buy—and the young ruler walked away empty. For everything, possessions and success, there is a price tag, and yes, there is a Mastercard. But for a life filled with God's righteousness, peace, love, and eternal life, priceless!

> Seek you first the kingdom of God and His righteousness and all these things will be added to you. (Matthew 6:33)

Cloud of Reflection

Reflect on your checkbook entries and write a prayer asking the Lord to help You place Him first.

Putting Your Faith in the Mail

Therefore I tell you, that everything
you pray and ask for-believe that you
have received it and it will be yours.

—Mark 11:24

Webster's definition of faith is a complete trust or confidence in someone or something. In this world of today, it is often difficult to find someone or something to have complete faith in. Oftentimes, we spend endless time and energy putting our faith in something or someone that will not produce what we want. The book of Hebrews says:

Faith is the reality of what is hoped for. The
proof of what is not seen. (Hebrews 11:1 NLT)

Think about the numerous times we display our faith on a daily basis. We insert a key in the ignition to start the car, we flip a switch to provide light, we insert a code to provide security, we drop a check or correspondence in a box for delivery are just a few illustrations. We don't stop and think that the car won't start, the lights won't come on, the security system won't arm or the mail will not be delivered. What if you inserted the key into the ignition but did not turn it or you touched the switch but did not flip it or opened the security panel without punching the code in or addressed and stamped correspondence but did not put it in the mailbox? None of this can be accomplished unless you let go. Correspondence written and not mailed does not do anything.

Real faith is letting go and trusting the source.

> Casting all your cares upon Him, for He
> cares for you. (1 Peter 5:7)

To have the faith that pleases Our God, the type of faith that produces peace in our hearts when we release our burdens, we must commit them to Him.

> Commit your way to the Lord, trust in Him
> and He will do this. (Psalm 37:5)

He will not work until we commit. We may believe in Him and ask of Him, but we will never fully receive His full blessing until we release and commit our burden. When we take our burdens and lay them at His feet but then pick them back up, we have displayed a lack of faith. How different our lives would be if we released our anxieties to our Lord as easily as we turn on a light switch or drop our mail in the mailbox? What burdens are you holding on to today? Release them. Drop them in the mail to be delivered to the One who is able to do all things.

Cloud of
Reflection

Make a God box. Find a box of any kind. Write your burdens on a piece of paper, only one each piece. Date it and then release it to the Lord. Then place in box.

Rainbow in the Clouds

I have set my rainbow in the cloud
and it shall be a sign of the covenant
between Me and the earth.

—Genesis 9:13

One of the most beautiful signs in God's creation is the rainbow. The traditional rainbow consists of seven colors: red, orange, yellow, green, blue, indigo, and violet. Meteorologists define rainbows as a phenomenon that is caused by a reflection and retraction of light in water droplets, resulting in a multi colored arc.

Our first account of the rainbow in the Bible is recorded in Genesis 9:13. God had sent a great flood to destroy mankind and all the sin. In verse fifteen, God promises never again to destroy the earth by flood, and verse sixteen says, "The rainbow shall be in the cloud, and I shall look on it to remember the everlasting covenant between God and every living creature of all flesh that is on this earth."

The rainbow is a symbol of God's grace and infinite mercy. When God judged sin with death, he then promised a Savior. The rainbow reminds us that God judges sin, but He is also merciful. John Gill in the *Exposition of the Bible* wrote that the rainbow is a bow without arrows and is not turned downward towards the earth but upward toward heaven, a token of endless mercy and love.

Judy Garland became popular in the movie, *The Wizard of Oz.* The song "Somewhere Over the Rainbow" is still played today. One of the verses goes like this:

> "Someday I'll wish upon a star. Way up where the clouds are far behind me. High above the chimney tops. That's where you will find me."

Children of God know that wishing upon a star is not going to put our clouds of difficulties behind us. We have a power that is greater than that—we have Jesus Christ, Savior of the world, the creator of the stars! He is able to move our clouds of difficulties behind us, although oftentimes He allows us to go through those clouds to get on the other side. The good news is we don't go alone. We have His power and presence with us. The rainbow is a symbol of God's promise that He will never leave us. Ezekiel 1:28 compares the rainbow to the radiance of Christ:

> As the rainbow appears that is in the cloud in the day or rain, so was the appearance of His brightness all around.

The next time you see a rainbow, reflect on God's mercy, faithfulness, and compassion.

Cloud of Reflection

List the times God has shown you His mercy. Write a verse to memorize to remind you of His faithfulness.

Real Protection

He shall cover you with His feathers, And
under His wings you shall take refuge.

—Psalm 91:4

Protection and being protected in today's world is a challenge more than ever. One can never assume that nothing will happen. It's imperative that you are aware of your surroundings at all times. ADT ran a commercial during Super Bowl 2019 with Jonathan and Drew Scott about what real protection is. They said, "Real protection is not about Ring doorbell, voice assistance or accessing your entire security system with one touch or checking your cameras inside and out. Real protection is much more. It's about have all this combined from the most trusted name in security, ADT." Living in the twenty-first century requires real protection.

David wrote in the ninety-first chapter of Psalms what real protection is and how to attain it. David wrote:

He who dwells in the shelter of the Most
High, will abide in the shadow of the Almighty.
And He who abides will have refuge and fortress.

Real protection. This protection is for those who love Lord God. In verses fourteen to sixteen, David provides us with eight things Lord God will do if we love Him.

Our Lord God will (1) rescue us, (2) protect us, (3) answer us, (4) be present in trouble, (5) deliver us, (6) honor us, (7) provide long life, and (8) show us salvation. Not one of these things will He do but all of them if we are His children and love Him. This protection for those who dwell under His wing. What a comfort to know as His children, we have security when we have a personal relationship with Our Lord Jesus.

In this day we live, we may have man-made protection; however, it is only temporary. True everlasting protection comes only from our living God. Choose today to punch in real security into the most trusted name in creation, Jesus Christ.

Cloud of
Reflection

Write on card the eight promises God said He would do and place in area to remind yourself daily.

Software versus Heart-ware

Guard your heart above all else,
for it is the source of life.

—Proverbs 4:23 (CSB)

Our world today is a technological world, and the foundation of the technology is software. Software is a set of instructions for computers to complete tasks. Software is essential for our TV, home security systems, automobiles, mobile phones, to list just a few. Software can be attacked and range from attacks on personal computers to the infrastructure of nations. The key to prevention of cyberattacks is antivirus programs requiring regular scans and updates. Software is the foundation for effectiveness in our technological life; however, our spiritual effectiveness is founded on our heart-ware.

Our heart-ware is the core of our spiritual being, enabling us to experience God's peace, joy, and love. Similar to software, our heart is vulnerable to virus attacks and requires regular scans and updates. These attacks can destroy our relationship with Jesus Christ. These attacks can appear in a variety of forms such as worry, pride, shame, greed, jealousy, anger, and more. Idols in our lives open the gate for viruses to attack us. Oftentimes, we do not recognize the virus attack because they generally step in small and quietly.

I personally struggle with worry, and I'm in a continual state of anxiety regarding the situations with my children and grandchildren. I pray and release them only to turn around in a few minutes to take them back. Does this sound familiar to anyone else? Worry is a lack of trust and separates our hearts from the peace and joy of the Lord. Jesus, in the tenth chapter of Luke, verses 41 and 42, reprimanded

Martha when she criticized her sister, Mary, for listening to Jesus and not working in the kitchen.

> And Jesus answered: "Martha, Martha, you are worried and troubled about many things. But one thing is needed and Mary has chosen that good part, which will not be taken away from her."

In the same way that computer software is protected by anti-virus programs, our hearts are protected with a shield of faith. Paul instructs the church at Ephesus, written in Ephesians 6:10–21 how to protect against spiritual warfare.

> Be strong in the Lord and put on the whole armor of God.

We are to stand firm with the belt of truth wrapped around us and put on the breastplate of righteousness. And above all, put on the shield of faith. When we pray, we are to pray continually and in the spirit. Spending time in God's presence and meditating on His word give us strength and the victory against the evil one.

> For I will go in the strength of the Lord God. (Psalm 71:16)

Our hearts are the source of our life, and Jesus commands us in Matthew 27:37 to "love the Lord your God with all your heart and with all your soul and with all your mind." When we love the Lord our God with all our heart, we are in the right place with Him. When is the last time you ran a scan and update on your heart? One of my favorite passages in Psalms is chapter 51, verses 10–12:

> Create in me a clean heart, O God, and renew a steadfast spirit within me. Do not cast me away from Your presence, And do not take

Your Holy Spirit from me. Restore to me the joy of Your salvation, And uphold me by Your generous Spirit.

Do not delay and protect your heart from the evil one and be filled with the Holy Spirit.

Cloud of Reflection

Write Psalm 51:10–12 as a prayer in your own words on an index card and place where you can read daily.

Stand By Me

The Lord stood by me and strengthened me.

—2 Timothy 4:7

"Stand by Me" is a popular soul classic first released by Ben E. King in 1961. It has been recorded and remade at least four hundred times by various artists such as John Lennon, The Drifters, Otis Redding to name a few. It was also done at the wedding of Prince Harry and Meghan Markle. According to King, the title is derived from and inspired by a spiritual written by Sam Cooke and J. W. Alexander called "Stand by the Father." The lyrics refer to the Bible passage in Psalm 46:5. The song talks about when the night has come and the land is dark, I won't be afraid as long as you stand by me. In chapter 46, verses 2–5:

> Therefore we will not fear though the earth
> gives way, though the mountains be moved into
> the sea, though it's waters roar and foam, though
> the mountains tremble at its swelling. God is in
> the midst of her; she shall not be moved.

We have the story of Moses in chapters 33 and 34 of Exodus encountering the presence of God. He asked God in chapter 33, verse 18, Moses said, "Please show me Your glory." The Lord answered that He would allow Him to see His back but not His face; however, He first instructed Moses to bring two tablets of stone and come to

Mount Sinai. Moses did as the Lord commanded him, and in verse 5, we have the account of Moses being in the Lord's presence.

> The Lord descended in a cloak and stood with him there and proclaimed the name of the Lord. The Lord passed before him and proclaimed, "The Lord, the Lord, a God who is merciful and gracious, slow to anger and abounding in steadfast love and faithfulness."

We have two important truths in this passage. One is God is Lord, not just a title but is the True Living God, and second, God is loving, faithful, and just. Moses sought out and longed for the presence of the Lord God, and the result was that the Lord stood with him.

The Lord wants us to seek His presence. He wants us to ask to see His glory. When the earth shakes and it is dark and everything around us is uncertain, the Lord, our God, is in our presence. The prophet Ezekiel ends his chapter calling out to "Jehovah-Shammah," the Lord is there. Our Lord will be there standing next to us, just as He did with Moses, and will reveal His glory when we seek Him. Jehovah-Shammah is with us in the dark and the light; we just have to call out to Him.

> The Lord is near to all who call upon Him,
> to all who call upon Him in truth. (Psalm 145:18)

Regardless if your skies are bright or dark, the Lord is there and stands beside you.

Cloud of Reflection

Reflect on a time when the Lord stood with you in a dark time. What did the Lord reveal to you during this time?

Stones Still Move

With man this is impossible, but
with God all things are possible.

—Matthew 19:26

In this journey we call life, we all have dealt with stones that weigh us down and block our progress. Stones of financial difficulty, broken relationships, addictions, and serious health issues are just a few. As I am writing this, I am quarantined at home in the middle of a pandemic outbreak of coronavirus. This pandemic is for sure a stone that is heavy and stopping progress. Actually, it is stopping life as we know it. Sports and concert events have been cancelled, and restaurants, bars, malls, and salons have been shut down. Travel unless necessary and only to domestic locations. People who are able are working from their homes; however, many others have been forced to file unemployment. As the outbreaks increase, the stock market decreases and demands for medical equipment increase. Overcoming this pandemic and returning to a normal lifestyle seem impossible.

There is the story of a woman who faced the impossible recorded in the gospel of Mark chapter 5, verses 25–34. This woman had been hemorrhaging for twelve years, resulting in a life quarantined from others because she was considered unclean. Her life was not moving forward, and this condition seemed impossible. What do we need to do in the middle of an impossible situation? We are to have faith, which is exactly what the woman in our passage did. She was desperate, but in her desperation, she reached out to Jesus. It is important

122

to note that faith takes us to Christ when we realize that we cannot resolve the problem and have no power. Faith requires obedience, bringing us to Christ resulting in peace and freedom.

Paul wrote in 2 Corinthians 4:18:

> So we do not focus on what is seen, but on
> what is unseen. For what is seen is temporary, but
> what is unseen is eternal.

Faith is God confidence that He will move the stones. The disciples also faced an impossible situation. The man they followed and called Lord was crucified, and their world stopped. The disciples were unable to move forward, and their hope was gone. Then the women went to the tomb of Jesus and looked up and saw that the stone had been rolled away. This is noted in Gospel of Mark 16:4. The same God that moved this stone still moves stones today. The pandemic will be over, and Our Lord will overcome.

What stone is stopping your progress today? Is it health, financial or relationship issues? Whatever the stone may be, release it to Our God, the creator of this universe who is able to do the impossible. Wait on him, and in His perfect time, He will move it.

> Now to Him who is able to do exceedingly
> abundantly above all that we ask or think, according
> to the power at work within us. (Ephesians 3:20)

Cloud of Reflection

Write down your stone and then write a prayer thanking God for moving it in His time.

Storm Surge

You will not need to fight this battle.
Stand firm, hold your position and
see the salvation of the Lord.

—2 Chronicles 20:17

Storms are a part of life. I live on the coast, and hurricane season is usually active. Meteorologists and their up-to-date technology alert us days ahead of the strength of storm, projected path, and models for landfall. This technology allows us to be prepared when the storm hits. However, there are storms in our lives that hit us unexpectedly, leaving us unsure of what to do next. These storms may be a natural disaster or a financial or health crisis. The pandemic of COVID in 2020 certainly left the entire world unprepared and unsure how to overcome the crisis.

Jehoshaphat, king of Judah, found in 2 Chronicles chapter 20, was confronted by a situation that appeared totally impossible to overcome. The Moabites and Ammonites were coming to battle against Judah, and the people ran to Jehoshaphat in fear. When he was alerted, he, too, was afraid and set his face to seek the Lord. Jehoshaphat asked God, "Aren't you the God of our Fathers, the God of heaven?" He affirms to himself that God was all powerful and had done many wonders. Jehoshaphat acknowledged the battle was too great and then the spirit of the Lord spoke:

Do not be afraid and do not be dismayed
at this great horde, for the battle is not yours but
God's. (2 Chronicles 20:16)

I love this story of Jehoshaphat taking action in the midst of an impossible situation. The key when we face impossible situations is to seek the Lord and to acknowledge that we are unable to fight this battle and He is all powerful. We need to focus on our God not on the storm.

The Lord God is in your midst, a mighty one to save; he will rejoice over you with gladness, he will quiet you with His love and he will exalt over you with singing. (Zephaniah 3:17)

Sometimes we receive alerts that a storm is approaching, and other times we are hit unexpectedly. Regardless how massive and powerful the storm is, we have a God who is more powerful. In Jeremiah 32:27:

Behold I am the Lord, the God of all flesh;
Is there anything too hard for me?

Satan wants us to believe the situation is impossible and give up. God does not ask us to fight the battle. He only asks us to stand firm, not be afraid, and to believe that God is able.

Verse 20:

Believe in the Lord your God and you will be established; believe his prophets and you will succeed.

Cloud of Reflection

If you are facing a storm today, ask the Lord to fight the battle for you. Memorize 2 Chronicles 20:17.

Take a Breath

The Spirit of God has made me, and the
breath of the Almighty gives me life.

—Job 33:4

As I am writing this, I am in the middle of the Christmas season, and finding time to take a breath is a challenge. Our daily lives are similar to treadmills. We set a pace, and before we know it, the hills and valleys have us panting and grasping for breath. The holiday season is definitely a time when catching our breath is sometimes difficult. We fill our hours with mailing cards, baking, shopping, wrapping, and parties, and oftentimes not stopping to enjoy the process. However, regardless of the time of year, we live life in a rush hour traffic mentality. We rush to work, rush home to cook dinner, rush to ball practices and meetings.

Breathing is essential for life, and we read in Genesis 2:7:

> Then the Lord God formed the man from
> the dust of the ground. He breathed the breath of
> life into the man's nostrils and the man became a
> living person.

We seldom think about the process of breathing. It just happens until we run into difficulty. When the weight of the world weighs down upon us, we struggle to take our next breath. Dealing with significant life changing events can make simple breathing out and in a challenge. During these times, we need to lean on our Heavenly Father who is able to do all things. The Lord God is our dwelling place, and He assists us to breath and trust Him. He doesn't expect us to fix the crisis, but He does expect us to trust Him. In Exodus 14:14:

> The Lord You God will fight for you.

Regardless of how difficult the situation, God is mighty and powerful. He will not leave us alone. The psalmists wrote in Psalm 3:4, "I cry to the Lord and He answered me from His holy mountain." On the days when the mountains will not move and you can't find a way around them, remember that God is near and has not abandoned you. "Do not be afraid or discouraged for the Lord your God is with you wherever you go."

On hard days, the best thing you can sometimes do is not think, not wonder, not imagine, not obsess but just breathe. Breathe in the Holy Spirit and breathe out fear, breathe in faith, and breathe out anxiety, breathe in peace, and breathe out conflict. Perhaps today you are having difficulty breathing because the mountains are so large and will not move. Stop and remember that the One who gave you the breath of life will help you to breathe.

Cloud of Reflection

Memorize Joshua 1:9.

The Christian Blueprint

Set your mind on things that are above
and not on things that are on earth.

—Colossians 3:2

Living in this world of chaos and continual change makes us vulnerable to Satan's seductions. At every corner, there are temptations to catch our eyes even if only for a moment. The media promotes living in the moment and attaining anything we want. So how can a Christian seduce proof and guard themselves from the snares of everyday life? Paul provided a blueprint for Christians to seduce proof their life in 1 Thessalonians 5:16–18.

1. Rejoice always. Be joyful. Joy and happiness are not synonyms. Happiness is based on our circumstances, whereas joy results when we abide in the Holy Spirit. The joy of the Lord sustains us during difficult circumstances.
2. Pray without ceasing. This means to be in a spirit of prayer. Life does not permit us to be on our knees all day; however, we can whisper prayers to Our Heavenly Father wherever we are working, shopping, driving. He hears our whispers and knows our need.
3. In everything, give thanks. Paul is not saying to be thankful for everything. It is unrealistic to be thankful for difficult times, however, we are to give thanks to God during those difficult times for His faithfulness and mercy. And we are to do this because it is the will of God.

4. Do not quench the Holy Spirit. Pray for the Holy Spirit to fill you, to direct you in the way you should go.

5. Do not despise prophecies. We should not make light of those who do not agree with us, but we should seek God's direction for whether those prophecies are true.

6. But test all things. Hold fast to God's Word. Check beliefs with God's Word. Only His word is true and right.

7. Abstain from every form of evil. Living in today's world makes it impossible to avoid every kind of evil; however, by walking in the Spirit, we can have the direction and the power we need to overcome evil

As you walk in this journey of life, beware of the seductions around you. Read this passage and apply it to your life.

> All scripture is given by inspiration of God, and is profitable for doctrine, for reproof, for correction, for instruction in righteousness that the man of God may be complete and thoroughly equipped for every good work. (2 Timothy 3:16)

Cloud of Reflection

Write these seven guidelines on an index card and place where you can review them daily.

The Great Eraser

As far as the east from the west so far He
has removed our transgressions from us.

—Psalm 103:12 (NKJV)

One of my special memories in elementary was my pencil box filled with new sharp pencils, scissors, crayons and most importantly, a large pink eraser. My Aunt Gerry, who was my second grade teacher, would tell us to use the pink eraser for the big mistakes. Oh goodness, how wonderful it would be to have a large pink eraser for our mistakes in our lives. We could use it erase our anger, bitterness, selfishness, unforgiveness, hurts, disappointments, and yes, our tears and pain. We could erase our significant mistakes that impact our life resulting in consequences. How much easier our lives could be if we could erase away the bad stuff and start over on a clean sheet of paper.

We live in a fix-it society. You make an accounting error on the bank statement, erase it, and it is fixed. When we lose our temper and say hurtful words then come back with "I'm sorry," and then the mistake is fixed. However, just as when I made a large mistake on paper and erased it, there were traces of the mistake on the paper. So is true for the mistakes we make in our lives. We may fix it, but depending on the severity of the mistake, oftentimes the traces remain.

Our Lord Jesus is our pink eraser. He is the greatest eraser of all. He is able to erase our mistakes and failures and provide us with a clean sheet of paper. God sent His son to erase our sins and provide His righteousness. Our scripture tells us He has removed our sins as far as the east is from the west. East and west can never meet, and this

130

illustrates how far God has removed our sin. He separates it from us and does not remembers it.

> If we confess our sins, He is faithful and
> righteous to forgive our sins and to cleanse us
> from all unrighteousness. (1 John 1:9 CSB)

It is awesome that God forgets our mistakes. Hebrews 10:17 in NLT translation states, "I will never again remember their sins and lawless deeds." What a wonderful promise! Many times the traces of our mistakes impact our lives, and we find it difficult to forget and move on.

One of the most effective tools Satan uses is to steal us of God's peace and joy by reminding us of our failures or hurts from others. We oftentimes relive them over and over in our minds. When we allow Satan to remind us of our mistakes, the lines are not erased, and we are unable to move on. Christ has erased our sins and mistakes, and while there may be scars and traces, we can move on in His strength. The author of Hebrews 12:1–2 (NKJV) states:

> Let us run with endurance the race that is
> set before us, looking unto Jesus.

The psalmist in Chapter 32:1:

> O what joy for those whose disobedience is
> forgiven, whose sin is put out of sight.

Today allow God to erase your mistakes and provide you with a clean sheet of paper and move forward with joy looking unto Jesus.

Cloud of Reflection

Journal an area that you need to allow Jesus to erase. Write a prayer asking the Lord to remove it and move on.

The Lord Is...

The Lord is My Shepherd, I shall not want.

—Psalm 23:1

The twenty-third psalms written by King David is probably one of the most familiar psalms. It is frequently used for funeral services. It is such a familiar passage that oftentimes we miss what it really means. Psalm 23 is more about how a person lives their life today rather than how to face death. It is a psalm that protects and provides us with strength every day and how to live in a personal relationship with Lord God. Psalm 23 is a blueprint on how to survive when storms are raging around us.

Psalm 23 is an active psalm for today's world. He makes me lie down in green pastures, He leads me beside still waters, He restores my soul, He guides me and is with me and anoints my cup. Nothing is past tense but present tense. The Lord, Yahweh, is the personal name of God and originates in the Hebrew language meaning I am. When we reflect on His attributes and power, it brings our focus to Him. I have been reflecting on the words "The Lord Is..." and have written several thoughts down.

The Lord is my shepherd, meaning that He will take care and guide me. The Lord is my light even in the darkness. Psalm 27:1:

The Lord is my light and my salvation.

Regardless of how dark the situation may seem, the light of the Lord's is with me. The Lord is gracious and righteous. Psalm 116:5:

> The Lord is gracious and righteous, our God full of mercy.

What an assurance that we have a God who is gracious and merciful in a world of ungracious and unmerciful people. The Lord is my refuge. What a comfort to know when the darkness falls upon us, we have a place to go—a place that will shelter us and protect us. Psalm 91:2:

> My refuge and my fortress, my God, in whom I trust.

My God will provide shelter during the storm. The Lord is my stronghold during the chaos and conflict of this world. When trials fall upon us, we have a stronghold with our Lord.
Psalm 27:1:

> The Lord is my stronghold of my life, of whom shall I be afraid?

The Lord is near to those who call upon Him. He never leaves us, and nothing can separate His children from His love. The Lord is good all the time even when we don't understand what He is doing. Psalm 145:9:

> The Lord is good to all, and His mercy is over all that he has made.

The Lord is my dwelling place, and underneath are His everlasting arms. The Lord is the creator. He is omnipresent, sovereign, and holy. The Lord is the difference in surviving life or nurturing in life. He is the difference in good times and bad. The Lord is my shepherd, and I have everything I need.

*Cloud of
Reflection*

Memorize the twenty-third Psalm.

The Lord's Prayer

Our Father in heaven hallowed be Your name.

Our Father, my Father, the creator of this universe, You have set the moon, stars and sun in
   their place. What an awesome God You are. Your name is above all names, holy and
   sovereign and righteous. Who am I that You love me?

Your kingdom come, and Your will be done on earth as it is in heaven.

Your kingdom reigns. No other kingdom is eternal. Guide me today to seek Your kingdom and
   not this earthly one. I ask for Your will to be done in all that I do today and for You to receive
   the glory.

Give us this day our daily bread.

I pray for what I need for today to live in Your spirit. You are the bread of life. Fill me today
   with the fruits of Your spirit, gentleness, patience, self-control, kindness, and joy.

And forgive us our debts as we forgive our debtors.

Forgive me, Father, for putting idols of this world ahead of You. Forgive me for my sins and
   help me to forgive others who hurt me. I pray today for a heart of forgiveness.

And do not lead me into temptation but deliver us from the evil one.

Guide me, Father, in the way I should go. It is so easy for me to walk into temptations. Grant me the power to overcome them. Thank you, Father, for Your plan and direction for me. I ask for your protection and deliverance from the chains of fear and evil.

For Yours is the kingdom and the power and the glory forever.

All the powers of this earth will bow to You, Oh God, I exalt and praise You for Your power, majesty, and glory. All things come from You. I praise You for Your faithfulness and unfailing love. Today, grant me the power to abide in You. Amen.

Cloud of Reflection

Write a prayer to God praising and thanking Him for all He is.

The Majesty and
Glory of His Name

O lord, our Lord, how majestic is
Your name in all the earth. You have
set Your glory above the heavens.

—Psalm 8:1

Niagara Falls is one of the most beautiful creations in the entire world. The falls consists of three waterfalls: the Horseshoe, the American, and the Bridal Veil. The combined falls form the highest flow rate of any waterfall in the world and have a vertical drop of more than a hundred and sixty-five feet. As I stood on the bridge, mesmerized by the enormous waterfalls, the words of a song our choir had sung many times came to my mind—"The Majesty and Glory of His Name." The psalmist in Psalm 8:3–4 says:

When I consider Your heavens, the work of
Your fingers, The moon and stars which You have
ordained. What is man that you are mindful of
him?

Only our God could create such a magnificent wonder. Oh Lord, our God, the majesty and glory of Your name! He is not just the creator of the beautiful Niagara Falls and this world, but He is also our creator! We may not consider ourselves to be as majestic and beautiful as Niagara Falls; however, in God's eyes, we are more beautiful and precious than all creation. Just as the falls display the majesty and glory of His name, I reflected about my life. Am I a reflection of His majesty and beauty in my everyday walk of life?

We are created for His glory, and our lives are to reflect His peace, greatness, mercy, and love. How do we achieve this? Spending time in His presence is necessary to be able to reflect His majesty. Reading His word, journaling, and thanking Him for our blessings give Him the glory to His name.

When we speak an encouraging word to some who are struggling or a generous act of kindness to someone in need, we reveal God's character of majesty and compassion. We should strive to reflect the glory and majesty of His name daily in our lives. Paul wrote to the Corinthian church in 1 Corinthians 10:31:

> Therefore whatever you do, do to the glory of God.

It doesn't matter how large or small the task is, do it to the best of your ability and give Him all the glory. The psalmist wrote in Psalm 68:34–35:

> Ascribe to the strength of God, His excellence is over Israel, And His strength is in the clouds, O God you are more awesome than Your holy places. The God of Israel is He who gives strength and power to His people.

Webster's definition of ascribe is to give credit to. We are to give credit to God for His power and marvelous works.

> Honor and majesty are before Him; strength and gladness are in His place. (1 Chronicles 16:27)

Reflect on God's creation and behold His majesty and glory and walk today in His presence reflecting His glory.

Cloud of
Reflection

Write down ways God shows you His majesty and glory.

The Real Church

They devoted themselves to the apostle's
teachings, to the fellowship and to the
breaking of bread and to prayer.

—Acts 2:42

Church statistics for 2017 reports that only 23 percent of Americans attend church regularly. The Gallup poll reports that 40 percent of Americans attend regular church services; however, that doesn't mean 49 percent are in church any given Sunday. The church is not only changing in numbers but also in the number of services, the type of music and activities, and the way people dress. I grew up going to church, and my mother made sure we always wore our very best dresses on Sunday and pants were not even considered. I have carried this tradition through all my adult life even though more women are dressed in pants than dresses. Where did this idea that we had to look our best come from? As I reflect on this, I have to honestly say that I spend more time on making myself look good on the outside than preparing my heart on the inside to worship.

We recently moved and have been searching for a new church, which is not an easy process; however, we have found a nondenominational church and absolutely love it! We were so caught up in worship that we didn't notice until after service that we were the only ones dressed up! My husband commented on the way home how refreshing it was to just worship and not check the program to see what came next. The fact that most attendees were in shorts and jeans did not stop the Holy Spirit. We have refused to change our dress in the past because we thought it mattered. WRONG. It doesn't matter. Our outward appearance is not relevant for worship, only our hearts.

Jesus rebuked the Pharisees and scribes in Matthew 23:25–28 about their outward appearance. He compared them to the white washed tombs in the cemetery. The tombs are beautiful on the outside but full of decay on the inside. Jesus is not interested in our outward appearance. He only cares about our heart.

> Do not let your adorning be external—the braiding of hair and the putting on of gold jewelry or the clothing you wear-but let your adorning be the hidden beauty of a gentle and quiet spirit which in God's sight is very precious. (1 Peter 3:3–4)

Real church is real worship as described in Psalms 138:1

> I will praise You with my whole heart; Before the gods I will sing praises to you. I will worship toward Your holy temple."

Real church is real worship focusing on the Almighty God, His holiness, grace and mercy. Yes, we do need to put on our "Sunday's Best" but not on the outside but inside our heart. The Lord looks on our inside and wants to change us and be glorified. As you prepare to attend church, spend more time preparing your heart than your appearance.

Cloud of Reflection

Find a scripture to prepare your heart for worship, write it down and memorize it.

The Real Identity

"I am the Alpha and the Omega," says
the Lord God, who is and who was
and who is to come, the Almighty.

—Revelation 1:8

Everyone has a sense of personal identity. Our personal identity includes life roles, attributes, and associations we consider important. This can be based on jobs, relationships, and associations such as an artist, policeman or lawyer. It is a sense of self, one's perception of self. We may not always know who we are, but we always know who we think we are. ID and driver's license cards document basic facts such as birthdate, height, weight, and address. Identification is essential in this lifestyle of today. Without proper identification, one cannot drive, vote, cash checks or travel on the airlines.

Life changing events often change who we think we are, for example, career changes. If you had asked me last year who I am, my response would have been, "I am a nurse." However, while I am still a nurse in my heart and soul, I am currently retired. And being an active nurse and a retired nurse are two different identifications. The role of a mother when a child is small is much different than the role of adult children. Lifestyles, roles, and relationships change as we become older; therefore, who we are changes. Sometimes accepting these changes are difficult, and we become unsure of who we are.

Jesus had no problem knowing who He was. Jesus tells His disciples in John 14:8:

I am the way, the truth and the life.

Jesus told the crowds of people, "I am the Son of God and whoever receives me as their Lord and Savior will have eternal life." There were no doubts for Jesus who He was. At the end of His journey on earth, when He prayed in the Garden of Gethsemane to His Father if there was another way but if not His will be done, Jesus was sure who of His role. In the fifteenth chapter of John, Jesus tells His disciples, "I am the true vine and My Father is the vinedresser." Jesus asks His disciples in Matthew 16:13, "Who do you say I am?" Peter replies, "You are the Christ, the son of the living God."

Peter experienced times in his life when he was not sure of himself or the events around him, but he was certain who Jesus was.

What an assurance we have in a time of constant change and chaos to have a God who never changes. He is and was and is to come, our living God. There are times in life's journey that we experience uncertainty about who we are and our role. Sudden events in our life can cause us to stumble and question who we are. These are the times not to remember who you are but instead who our God is. Regardless of our lifestyles and roles that change, He will complete the work he started.

Being confident of this very thing that He
who has begun a good work in you will complete
it until the day of Jesus Christ. (Philippians 1:6)

Casting Crown has a song entitled "Who Am I?" and the chorus says:

Not because of who I am but because of
what have done
Not because of what I have done but because
of who You are.
He told me who I am, I am Yours.

Cloud of
Reflection

Reflect on who Jesus is to you.

Write down words that describe who He is personally to you.

The Right Stronghold

The Lord is the stronghold of
my life, whom shall I fear?

—Psalm 27:1

Most of us have strongholds in our life that we are constantly in battle with. Exactly what is a stronghold? The dictionary defines it as a place that is fortified and safe. Paul defines spiritual strongholds in 2 Corinthians 10:5 as any argument or belief that sets itself up against the knowledge of God. It is anything that exalts itself in our mind and takes over our focus on God. A stronghold in this reference is not a fortress of safety but a place of destruction. Stronghold comes in various sizes and shapes. It may be an addiction, hatred, pride or anger. Regardless of the type of strongholds, the result is the same—it consumes our mind, stealing our emotional and physical strength, resulting in a faith that is ineffective.

However, there is a stronghold that is right and safe—Our Lord God. David knew the Lord God was his stronghold. In 2 Samuel 22:2–3, he wrote to the Lord on the day the Lord rescued him from his enemies:

The Lord is my rock, my fortress, my God,
my stronghold, my refuge.

Nahum wrote to the people of Judah in chapter 1, verse 7:

The Lord is good, a stronghold in the day
of trouble.

150

One of my favorite authors, Beth Moore, wrote a book about breaking free from strongholds, *Praying God's Word*. The only way to break free of those strongholds that hold us in bondage is to release them to the one and only true stronghold, Lord Jesus. Paul tells us in 2 Corinthians 10:5 how by turning aside every thought into captivity to the obedience of Christ, God's weapons of prayer, hope, faith, and love are able to overcome any stronghold that we have.

> He is my faithful love and my fortress, my
> stronghold and my deliver. (Psalm 144:2)

Whatever stronghold you have in your life that steals your spiritual energy and makes your faith powerless, release them to the One who overcomes all evil sand conquers all.

*Cloud of
Reflection*

List strongholds in your life. Write a scripture to help you overcome it and pray this verse.

Throw Out the Anchor

We have this hope as an anchor
for the soul, firm and secure.

—Hebrews 6:19a

Webster's definition of an anchor is a heavy object attached to a rope or chain to secure a vessel to the bottom of the sea. The word *anchor* is often used metaphorically to represent God and faith. An anchor secures us and makes us steadfast. As children of God, we have an anchor that never fails when the storms of life rush upon us. Anchors are things that make us feel grounded and secure and can be a person, place or thing. Our anchors in our life can be our job or perhaps a spouse. Some anchors for others are their home where they feel safe and protected. There are many examples of anchors that make us feel secure; however, there are times in our life when those anchors we hold on to are unable to sustain us during a storm. The only anchor strong enough is our Lord God, Jehovah!

The author of Hebrews in chapter 6, verses 13–20 was writing to people who were facing hardship and persecution because of their Christian faith. He is encouraging them to place their focus on the promises of God—the promises that will anchor our life during the storm and not fail. The author in verse 19 uses the metaphor of an anchor that does not go to the bottom of the ocean but goes up into the heaven behind the veil where Jesus first entered for us and our salvation.

We have this as a sure and steadfast anchor of the soul, a hope that will not fail. This passage in chapter 6 tells us that God has gone the extra mile in seeing to it we have strong encouragement to hold fast to our hope in Him. In verse 18, God takes an oath in order to assure us that He has secured a future for us, and He does not lie.

> For I know the plans I have for you, declares
> the Lord, plans for your welfare, not for evil, to
> give you a future and a hope. (Jeremiah 29:11)

Paul wrote in Acts chapter 27 about the storm at sea along the island of Crete. When the storm began to drive them across the Adriatic Sea, they dropped four anchors and prayed. What is our reaction when the storm in life drive us into a mountain that will not move? Do we drop to our anchor, Jesus, and pray or do we panic and try to find a way around the mountain?

Abraham believed that God's promises were true and waited patiently regardless of how impossible it seemed. You may have a storm in your life that looks impossible, a mountain that you are unable to go around. Throw out your anchor to Jehovah, the Lord your God! He knows the way and will keep you on course even when you can't see the course. The battle song of the US Navy is "Anchors Aweigh," and the lyrics are to throw out the anchor and go fight the battle.

We have a high priest who will fight the battle for us. We just have to let go and trust Him. Hold on to the anchor that will not let go. What anchors are you holding to? The earthly ones or the heavenly one, Jesus, who will not fail?

> For in this hope we were saved. Now hope
> that is seen is not hope. For who hopes for what
> he sees? (Romans 8:24)

Today I challenge you to throw out your worries and fears and anchor to the Lord God.

> May the God of hope fill you with all joy and
> peace in believing so that by the power of the Holy
> Spirit you may abound in hope. (Romans 15:13)

Cloud of
Reflection

Write one promise from God and memorize it.

To God Be the Glory
(In All that We Do)

Ascribe to the Lord the glory due
His name, worship the Lord in
the splendor of His holiness.

—Psalm 29:2

Our key verse is very specific about our role in our relationship with Christ. We are to ascribe to the Lord the glory that He deserves. In the KJV, the translation is "give to the Lord." The definition of ascribe is to credit or assign, to give to a source or cause. The application of this verse is to humbly acknowledge God for His characteristics. In everyday language, give credit where credit is due.

Interesting that the words ascribe and worship are in the same verse. First, we are to give Him the credit that belongs to Him, and second, we are to worship in the presence of His holiness.

Our God is holy and majestic, sovereign above all.

Blessed be His glorious name forever, may the whole earth be filled with His glory. (Psalm 72:19)

I don't know about you, but for me, it is easy to go before the Lord with all my concerns and not ascribe or give him praise. You may ask how do I give Him glory due His name. Simply by worshipping and spending time in His presence.

> Oh Lord, our Lord, how majestic is Your name in all the earth. (Psalm 8:1)

Our God deserves our praise and worship.

> To Him belong glory and dominion forever and ever. (1 Peter 4:11)

Ascribe to Him glory and worship His holiness.

Cloud of Reflection

Write a praise to Our Lord giving Him the glory.

True Love Revealed

By this we know love because He
laid down His life for us.

—1 John 3:16

Valentine's Day—a specific holiday set aside to tell and show those close to us that we love them. Valentine's Day is a day of celebration of love and affection. One legend contends that Valentine was a priest who served during the third century in Rome. When Emperor Claudius II determined that single men made better soldiers than those married, he outlawed marriage for young men. Valentine defied Claudius and performed marriages for young lovers in secret. When he was finally discovers, Claudius had Valentine put to death.

There are other tales regarding Valentine's Day, but through the years, it has remained to be a popular holiday celebrated across the world. Chocolates, stuffed animals, and flowers are sold everywhere. Valentine's cards filled the racks with every possible message of love you can imagine. Children of all ages decorate a variety of Valentine's cards for their family and friends.

Valentine's Day—a day of love. True love, real love in the times we live in, is difficult to find. True love is not about cards, flowers, and candy but about the feelings one person has for another. Valentine's Day is about revealing love for someone. God provided us the perfect example of revealing love.

For God so loved the world, that He gave
His only begotten Son, that whoever believes

in Him, should not perish but have eternal life.
(John 3:16)

True love revealed a love that is unconditional and everlasting. Paul defines love in the thirteenth chapter of 1 Corinthians verses 4–7:

> Love is patient and kind; love does not envy or boast; it is not arrogant or rude. It does not insist on its own way; it is not irritable or resentful; it does not rejoice at wrongdoing but rejoices with truth. Love bears all things, believes all things, hopes all things and endures all things.

God revealed true love when He sent His son to die for our sins and give us an everlasting life.
1 John 4:9:

> In this love of God was made manifest among us, that God sent His only Son into the world, so that we might live through him.

In verse 7, John tells us that we are to love one another for love comes from God. And if we don't love, we don't know God because God is love. Our Father's love is not about flowers and candy that will perish but about a love that will never perish. God's love is merciful, gracious, and full of compassion not just one day a year but every day for those who are children of God. Jesus commands us to love as His Father loves. The first two commandments that God revealed to Moses was first to Love the Lord you God, and the second was to Love your neighbor as you love yourself.

In chapter 3 of 1 John verse 18, "Little children, let us not love in word or talk but in deed and truth." We love because He first loved us—true love revealed. A love that is able to conquer all things. A love that will not perish. As children of the King, we are to reveal the true love of God to those around us. Paul says it so perfectly in the thirteenth chapter of 1 Corinthians:

> So now abide faith, hope and love, these
> three; but the greatest of these is love.

Cloud of Reflection

List ways you can reveal God's true love to others.

Turtle Preciseness

Therefore we are surrounded by such a huge
crowd of witnesses to the life of faith, let us
strip off every weight that slows us down,
especially the sin that so easily trips us up.
We do this by keeping our eyes on Jesus.

—Hebrews 12:1–2 (NLT)

One of my favorite workouts is running. I have not run a marathon but have completed several five- and ten kilometer-runs. Through the years, running has become more challenging; however, my goal is always to complete the race without walking. In order to accomplish this goal, I set my pace slow and steady, just like the turtle. The turtle is a symbol of the Native Americans, representing Mother Earth. It signifies health, perseverance, and longevity.

God's Word talks about running the race and instructs us how to run with endurance and perseverance just like the turtle. The prophet Isaiah spoke to the children of Israel in Isaiah 40:31:

But those who wait upon the Lord shall
renew their strength…they shall run and not be
weary; they shall walk and not faint.

There are three guidelines in our key verse for completing the race and achieving the prize. First, we are to remember the cloud of witnesses. For example, Abraham, Noah, Sara, and Elijah who were faithful and completed the race, receiving the prize. Reflect on the people in your life who have made an impact on your Christian journey with their perverseness and faithfulness. They encourage us to continue on the course, slow and steady.

Second, we are to throw off the sin that weighs us down and causes us to trip. In the ancient days, the runners would tie up their robes so they would not trip. We are surrounded by snares at every turn on our race. Paul wrote to the church of Corinth in 1 Corinthians 9:24–27 to run to obtain the prize. He went on to say that every athlete exercises self-control to complete the race. As we travel on this journey called life, we must consciously discard the sins of the world so we can obtain the prize. I found this quote form Winston Churchill:

> Continuous effort, not strength or intelligence, is the key to unlocking our potential.

And the last guideline is to fix our eyes upon Jesus. When we turn our eyes to the world for solutions to our circumstances, we start to stumble and fall. As long as Peter kept his eyes on Jesus, he was able to walk across the water; however, when he turned his eyes from Jesus to his circumstances, he started to sink. We must run the race with our eyes upon Jesus. In Philippians 3:13, Paul wrote to the church of Philippi:

> But I focus on one thing: Forgetting the past and looking forward to what lies ahead, I press on to reach end of the race and receive the heavenly prize.

We need to set our pace slow, steady, and precise. The turtle teaches us that everything you are and everything you need to complete the race is inside you, and you carry it with you. As children of the King, we have everything we need to complete the race and obtain our heavenly prize. Reflect on those who have ran the race before us and obtained the prize. Throw away sins that trip us up and keep our eyes focused on Jesus.

Cloud of
Reflection

Journal what slows you down in your race and write a prayer for the Lord to help you.

Uh-Oh Cloud Alert!

Moses approached the thick
darkness where God was.

—Exodus 20:21

Our human nature prefers light and sunshine; however, life consists of both sunshine and clouds, light and darkness. Our favorite days are those filled with blue skies rather than the days that are cloudy and gray. Thick clouds of darkness are fearful to us. In Exodus 20:18–21, we read that the children of Israel witnessed the thunder, lightning and the smoking mountain and dark thick clouds and were afraid. They backed away, but Moses drew near to the thick darkness where God was. In that dark thick cloud, God spoke to Moses, revealing His law and power.

Our God often take us into thick clouds of darkness to instruct us. It may be a cloud of grief, illness or depression. In the clouds of darkness, God is our refuge. David wrote in Psalm 91:1:

He who dwells in the shelter of the Most
High will rest in the shadow of the Almighty.

In the cloud, God removes the glare of the world so we can hear His voice. The noise of this world makes it difficult to focus in God's presence. Moses showed us the example to approach the cloud and enter in and listen to the voice of the Almighty. Do not be afraid to enter the darkness for God is in there and with you and on the other side of the darkness is His radiant light.

For Your mercy reaches unto the heavens,
And Your truth unto the clouds. (Psalm 57:10)

Is there a cloud over you today? Maybe it is a temptation too difficult to resist or a heavy burden. Do not be afraid and approach the cloud and listen to the Lord your God. The Lord will reveal His truth, righteousness and light.

What I tell you in the dark, speak in the
light. What you hear in a whisper, proclaim on
the housetops. (Matthew 10:27 CSB)

Approach your cloud and see the power and glory of God.

Exodus 16:10:

They looked toward the desert, and there
was the glory of the Lord appearing in the cloud.

*Cloud of
Reflection*

Memorize Joshua 1:9.

Wave Effect

"Let the heavens be glad and the earth
rejoice! Let the sea and everything
in it shout His praise!"

—Psalm 96:11 (NLT)

Spending time at the beach and watching the waves crash upon the sand are something I never grow tired of. A wall of water forms way out in the ocean and rushes upon the shore disrupting sand and shells. The waves are in perpetual motion, carrying shells and debris out to the ocean floor. This continuous process removes the debris and leaves the shore refreshed and renewed. Time at the beach is always therapeutic for me. The stresses of life often leave me feeling overwhelmed and trapped.

When I sit on the beach and gaze out into the ocean, I am released by the restrictions of life. As far as I can see is the ocean and sky—no limits! Just as the waves redesign and renew the shore, the same is true for us when we allow God's waves of mercy and grace to wash over us. He removes the debris of my life: the failures, disappointments, and stains from sin. His mercy and grace removes our negative attitudes and bitterness when we sit still in His presence.

The voice of the Lord is upon the waters, the God of glory thunders. The Lord thunders over the mighty seas. The voice of the Lord is powerful; the voice of the Lord is majestic. (Psalm 29:3–4)

The beach is redesigned as a result of the continuous motion of the waves upon the sand. In the same way, the Holy Spirit designs us. His unfailing love renews us. The oceans is always at work on the shore as he tides ebb and flow reshape and refreshes it. Likewise, the Holy Spirit is always at work in us, renewing us with God's mercy and grace. During seasons of our life when we are overwhelmed and discouraged, we need to come into the presence of the Holy Spirit. In Psalm 42:6–8:

> Now I am deeply discouraged, but I will remember you. I hear the tumult of the raging sea. As your waves and surging tides sweep over me, But each day the Lord pours His unfailing love upon me.

Today stop and be still. Come into His presence and allow His grace, mercy, and love to cleanse and renew your life.

Cloud of Reflection

Memorize a verse that is about God's unfailing love.

What is in your Backpack?

Then Jesus said: "Come to me, all
you who are weary and carry heavy
burdens, and I will give you rest."

—Matthew 11:28

Backpacks are a popular item today, which is used for travel, school, and hiking, to name a few. The first backpack was created in 1878 and was a combination of wood and canvas. In 1938, Jerry Cunningham added a zipper and used nylon instead of canvas. Backpacks are essential for hiking trips. The backpack should contain essential items such as water, protein bars, first aid kit, insect repellent, knife, survival gear, lighter, toilet paper, zip lock bags, and of course, a map and compass. The weight of backpack should not be more than 20 percent of your body weight.

What about your backpack that you carry each day? Is it packed with the essentials for a successful day or is it heavy and weighs you down? In this journey of life, we can start out with a lightweight backpack, but as our day progresses, we often find our backpack heavy with frustration, discouragement, anger, and despair. Just as important as packing our backpack for a hiking trip, it is important to pack our backpack for this road trip of life with essentials.

Let's discuss what some of the essentials for our backpack are. One of the first items I think of is joy. Not the joy that results from receiving something we want, but true joy that comes from the love of God—joy that is not determined by our circumstances.

> In Your presence there is fullness of joy.
> (Psalm 16:11b)

And 1 Chronicles 16:27:

> Splendor and majesty are before him;
> strength and joy are in his place.

Biblical joy is choosing to respond to external circumstances with an inner contentment and satisfaction because we know that God will use these experiences to accomplish His work in and through our lives. The source of our joy is God, our Lord. Having godly joy provides us with the strength we need on this journey.

> For the joy of the Lord is your strength.
> (Nehemiah 8:10)

Another essential for our backpack is forgiveness. Colossians 3:13 states:

> Bearing with one another, and if one has a
> complaint against another, forgiving each other;
> as the Lord has forgiven you, so also must forgive.

We have all encountered people who have treated us wrong and unfairly. It can be very difficult to forgive that person; however, that is exactly what Jesus tells us to do. A forgiving spirit in our backpack allows us to have joy, peace, and the ability to experience life without bitterness.

Item number three is patience, and I do not know about you, but this one is the hardest oftentimes for me. We live in a society that endorses instant gratification and get it quick. Patience is not a quality that is easily attainable, at least for me. I become easily frustrated with slow drivers, waiting on medical reports, red lights to turn green or waiting for Wi-Fi to connect.

Proverbs 15:18:

> Hot tempers cause arguments, but patience
> brings peace.

Patience keeps our backpack light and frees us. And in the book of Ecclesiastes 7:8, "The end of something is better than its beginning. Patience is better than pride." Paul tells us that patience is a fruit of the spirit and the result of Christ living in us. And along with patience, we need to pack self-control. There are days it takes a lot of self-control for me not to tell that child that I have had it or to slam down the phone on a sales representative who is not listening to me. We need self-control to balance our lives.

The next item would be kindness, and in this self-centered society we live in, there is not enough of it! We all want to be treated with kindness; however, all you have to do is read the news or social media and see all the meanness that is written. It is not okay to be unkind on social media regardless if the person deserves it. We become so wrapped up in our desires and agenda that oftentimes, we forget to show kindness. Acts of kindness can be as simple as a smile, thank you, holding the door for someone or sending a card to cheer someone.

Peace is another essential item for our backpack, especially in this chaotic world, which we live in. You may ask how do we have peace when politicians are constantly fighting, natural disasters occurring regularly, and our jobs and family demand our constant attention. David wrote in the thirty-seventh chapter of Psalms verse one, "Fret not yourselves because of evildoers, but trust in the Lord, and do good."

David goes on to say in verse 7, "Be still and wait patiently for him." The ability to have peace is recorded in Isaiah 26:3:

> You keep him in perfect peace whose mind
> is stayed on you, because he trusts you.

The last item for our backpack is love and the most important of all.

> So not faith, hope, and love abide, these
> three, but the greatest of these is love. (1
> Corinthians 13:13)

Love conquers all, and without love, we are unable to experience the joy and fullness of Christ. With love, we are able to be patient and kind and forgiving. When Jesus was asked what the greatest commandment is, he replies: "Love the Lord your God with all your heart and with all you should and with all you mind. This is the first and greatest commandment. And the second is to love your neighbor as yourself." Christ's love empowered in us by His Holy Spirit that keeps our backpack light and enables us to share His glory with others.

So what's in your backpack? Is it bitterness, anger, impatience, unforgiveness or is it joy, forgiveness, kindness, peace, and love? Start your day by packing the essential, and end your day by unpacking the items that have weighed you down and slowed your process. The best part about being a child of God is that He provides new mercies every morning, and His steadfast love never changes recorded in Lamentations 3:22:

> The Steadfast love of the Lord never ceases;
> His mercies are new every morning.

Cloud of Reflection

Evaluate your backpack and write down what you need to remove and what item to you need to add.

When the Darkness Falls

And I will give you treasures hidden
in the darkness, secret riches, so that
you may know that I am the Lord.

—Isaiah 45:3a

Most of us, if given a choice, would choose light over dark. We prefer days filled with sunshine versus those filled with dark clouds and rain. In the beginning, the earth was formless, and darkness covered the water. Then God said, "Let there be light," and He separated the light from the darkness (Genesis 1:2-4).

Our Creator wanted there to be both light and dark, so He created day and night. And He also allows light and dark in our daily lives as well according to His perfect plan. There are times we experience the veil of darkness falling upon us. During the darkness, it is difficult to find our way back to the light. At the time of writing this, our earth just experienced a total solar eclipse for the first time in ninety-nine years. Weeks prior to this event, the media talked about the best places to be, where to buy solar glasses, and what to look for. Social media joined in the posting of eclipse parties. The sun is swallowed by the moon for a brief time, and as the moon passes between the earth and sun, its shadow is cast upon the earth. Gazing at the sun during the eclipse is harmful, and we need solar filters to protect our eye. The same is true for us when darkness falls upon us. Just as it is harmful to stare at the sun during the eclipse, our vision is damaged when we stare in the darkness. We need the filter of the Son Jesus Christ to move us into the light.

Darkness had fallen upon the children of Israel. The cities were desolate, and the people were captive to the Babylonian empire. The result of pagan worship and idolatry had corrupted their hearts. Isaiah warned the people repeatedly to return to God. In chapter 45, the Lord anointed Cyrus to lead his children out of the darkness, and in verse 2, God says, "I will go before you and level the uneven places, I will shatter the bronze doors and cut the iron bars in two."

The Almighty God will even out the rough places and bring us out of the darkness. In verse 3:

> I will give you the treasures of darkness and
> secret riches from secret places, so that you may
> know I am the Lord.

The treasure of darkness and secret riches refers to the vanquished pagan nation who had hid their wealth in vaults. This passage can apply to us when the veil of darkness falls upon us. During this dark time, God will provide us with His treasures—treasures of mercy, strength, compassion, and power of His presence. God's purpose is the same for us as the children of Israel, and that is to show us that He is the Lord and will lead us to His light.

God has our attention in the darkness and wants us to know His power and glory. We are in the dark by God's plan and timing, and during this time, we are to put on glasses of faith to protect our spiritual vision.

> Lord, you light my lamp, my God illumi-
> nate my darkness. (Psalm 18:28)

So my friends, when, not if, the darkness falls upon you, use your faith eyes to find God's treasures. The psalmist in Psalm 112:4 tells us that "light shines in the darkness for the upright, He is gracious, compassionate and righteous. And in verse 6 tells us that we will not be shaken."

Cloud of Reflection

Reflect on a time you were in the darkness. Write what treasure did God reveal to you.

Whirlpool or Whirlwind

As for me, I look to the Lord for help, I
will wait confidently for God to save me,
and my God will certainly save me.

—Micah 7:7 (NLT)

Our lives can be compared to the ocean tide—highs and lows. One day everything is flowing together, and the next day, nothing will connect properly. We know that trials produce perseverance character and character and hope. God's word in James 1:2 states:

Count it all joy, my brothers, when you
meet trials of various kinds.

We are not to rejoice in the difficulty; however, we are to rejoice in what God will do. Paul writes in 2 Corinthians 12:9 that in our weakness, God's power and glory are made perfect. The Lord uses these times of low tides to sanctify me and lift me higher. These times are when God can direct and guide me because he has my attention.

However, the key to receiving what God desires is our response. We have a choice of choosing to be like a whirlwind or a whirlpool—A whirlpool, which is a rapidly rotating mass of water pulling us downward, a mass of fears spiraling us into anguish and darkness, into a mass of hopelessness. There is no peace and only despair and fear.

Or we can choose the whirlwind response. This response is founded on faith regardless of the circumstances. Romans chapter four describes the faith of Abraham:

> He did not waver at the promise of God
> through unbelief, but was strengthen in faith giv-
> ing glory to God. (Romans 4:20)

Abraham was convinced that God was able and faithful to His promises. A whirlwind faith will lift us upward and outward, resting on God's promises, and the result is peace, hope, and joy instead of fear and despair.

Our lives are marked seasons of low and high tides. When the low tides comes, will you choose to respond like the whirlpool or the whirlwind? My prayer is to be like the whirlwind and be lifted high and filled with God's joy and peace.

> For we walk by faith, not by sight. (2 Cor-
> inthians 5:7)

Cloud of Reflection

Find a promise from God. Journal what this specific promise means personally.

X Marks the Spot

Therefore know that the Lord your God, He is
God; the faithful God who keeps covenant and
mercy for a thousand generations with those
who love Him and keep His commandments.

—Deuteronomy 7:9

Everywhere we turn, there are markers to let us know where we are
and what we are doing. Markers on maps enable us to arrive at the
correct location. Our roadways are lined with signs marking exits,
attractions, gas stations, and restaurants. Markers not only mark our
location but also our progress or accomplishments.

I love to watch the Olympic Games. The 2016 Games was filled
with amazing athletes in all events. The women's gymnastics team in
2016 took over the events, exceling above all expectations. This team
of young women won the hearts of not only Americans but the entire
world. The judges would deduct marks for any mistake, and every
mark made a difference in the placement in the events.

In the third and fourth chapters of Joshua is the story of the
children of Israel passing through the River Jordan. The children
walked across the Jordan River on dry land. The crossing was proof
that God is in control and able to do all things. As the priests carried
the ark into the Jordan, the waters stopped flowing allowing the people to cross over. God then instructed Joshua to have the Israelites to
set up twelve stones. Each stone represented a tribe. These markers
were a reminder of God's power not only to the ones present but also
for generations to come. However, the real point is not the stones
marking the spot. The significance of the markers was to remind

the children of Israel when they faced difficulties and failures of the power of God. The stones marked what God had done in their lives, what only God could do. The stones are a reminder that nothing is impossible with God.

Jesus tells His disciples in John 5:17, "My Father has been working until now and I have been working."

Jesus was predicting His death and resurrection. God is always working in our lives. He will not stop until He completes the good work He started.

> For I am confident that He who began a
> good work in you will perfect it until the day of
> Jesus Christ. (Philippians 1:6)

What stones represent and mark what God has done on your journey of life? We are often so busy on our journey that we fail to recognize God's work and power. Identifying the stones in our life that marks God's power helps us not only to see what He has done, but in times of trials and difficulties, it reminds us that He is able. All things are possible with Him.

Cloud of Reflection

List twelve "stones" in your journey that mark what God has done in your life. Keep them accessible, and when trials come, review them. Reflect on God's presence and power and faithfulness

You are My Sunshine

The light shines in the darkness, and
the darkness has not overcome it.

—John 1:5

Sunshine—how we thrive on it! Regardless of what is happening around us, when the sun is shining, we are able to move forward. I love the days on the lake when the sun beams down on the water, making it sparkle! While we know that rain is essential for our environment and growth, we, at least most of us, prefer the sunshine.

Recently we experienced twelve days straight of rain and clouds. I kept telling myself we needed it and went through the motions of thanking God until day three. I attempted to write and study, but my spirit was so heavy that I just gave up. When it finally stopped and the sun came out, I was elated, and my spirit was high as the sky. I praised God for the bright warmth. *This is what I needed, Lord!* And I heard his voice ever so softly, *You needed the rain too, my child.*

On the sunshine days when our world is going our way, we rush about confident and content and full of energy and motivation. Oh, but when the rain comes, that is a different story. It may be a light rain such as an auto repair, the washing machine crashes or we have a conflict at work or school. And then there are huge storms that rock our foundation. Where is the sun? The light to give us strength and hope. The sun is still there, behind the dark clouds. Our Lord Jesus, THE Son, is present in the darkness. He is the light and hope.

David in chapter 18, verse 30, "This God—his way is perfect, the word of the Lord proves true and He is a shield for all those who take refuge in Him."

And in verse 39, "For You have equipped me with strength for the battle." Our Lord knows our struggles during the rainy days, and He has provided everything we need not to just survive but also to grow according to His plan. And when the storm is over, He provides us with sunshine and rainbows to remind us He has not forsaken us and He is sovereign.

The weather today for you may be bright and sunny, and life is good. Or the weather for you today may be rainy and dark with clouds, and life is hard. Regardless, The Son of Our God, Creator of this universe, is present and in full control. Our Father is our sunshine even in the storms. Trust Him. His way is perfect. Nothing is impossible for God, and He is always in our midst.

*Cloud of
Reflection*

Today, regardless of sunshine or clouds, write down something you are thankful for.

About the Author

Jan Marie Oakley grew up in Southeast Texas and attended Lamar University and graduated from School of Nursing in 1973. She specialized in geriatric nursing and retired after forty-three years of service.

As a nurse, wife, mother, grandparent, teacher, mentor, and friend; God has used Jan's insight into His Word to touch the lives of many. Her knowledge of nursing and healthcare is coupled with her genuine love for people. Her journey through life and commitment to helping others has opened a variety of doors of ministry such as leading Alzheimer's Support group for caregivers, card ministry, and presenting training seminars for nurses.

Jan and her husband live in Dallas, Texas, with their dog Dixie. They have three children and two grandchildren. They love boating and frequently host a neighborhood Bible study in their home. Writing a devotional book was a goal that Jan has had for a long time.